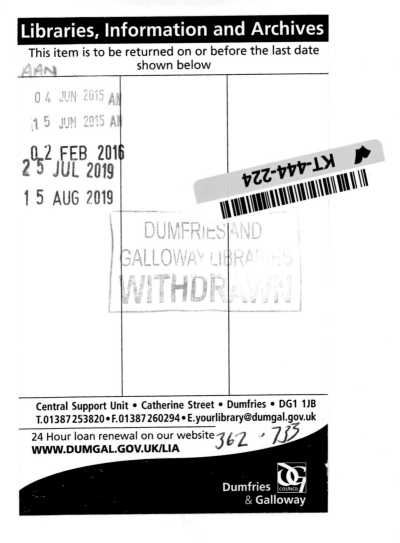

Nowhere
to Go

BY THE SAME AUTHOR:

The Boy No One Loved
Breaking the Silence
Crying for Help
The Girl Without a Voice
Just a Boy
A Last Kiss for Mummy
Little Prisoners
Mummy's Little Helper
Too Hurt to Stay

CASEY WATSON

SUNDAY TIMES BESTSELLING AUTHOR

Nowhere to Go

The heartbreaking true story of a boy
desperate to be loved

HarperElement
An Imprint of HarperCollins*Publishers*
77–85 Fulham Palace Road,
Hammersmith, London W6 8JB

www.harpercollins.co.uk

First published by HarperElement 2014

1 3 5 7 9 10 8 6 4 2

© Casey Watson 2014

Casey Watson asserts the moral right to
be identified as the author of this work

A catalogue record of this book is
available from the British Library

PB ISBN 978-0-00-754308-3
EB ISBN 978-0-00-754309-0

Printed and bound in Great Britain by
Clays Ltd, St Ives plc

FSC™ ... note
the resp ... the
FSC lab ... ome
fro ...

Find out more about HarperCollins and the environment at
www.harpercollins.co.uk/green

Dedicated to all those in a position to help our children lead productive and fulfilling lives, and to those children who have lived through dark days and find the strength to make it.

Acknowledgements

I would like to thank my agent, the lovely Andrew Lownie, for continuing to believe in me; Carolyn and the wonderful team at HarperCollins for their dedicated and hard work; and as ever my very talented friend and mentor, Lynne, for always being there. A special mention this time to Vicky at HarperCollins, who is taking some special time out for a while. I wish her all the very best and look forward to hearing from her soon.

Chapter 1

It's so easy to take your parents for granted, isn't it? Not consciously, maybe, and not in the sense that you don't value them. Just in that perhaps it goes with the territory that you try not to spend too much time thinking ahead to a time when they won't be there, do you? But not today. Today I had no choice in the matter. So I was doing exactly that, and it was scary.

I was scared because I had just taken my father into hospital to have major surgery on his bowel. It would be straightforward, they told us, and we should try not to worry, but how can you not in that situation? Mum was terrified he might die under the anaesthetic – i.e. before they even started – and for all my reassurances and positivity, she had so many 'what if?' scenarios (all of them negative, obviously) that it had been a real job to try and keep her calm.

As it was, I'd left her there with her knitting – she was busy making a cot blanket for her newest great-grandchild

– and the promise that I'd be back as soon as Dad was out of theatre, after which, assuming all was well, I'd bring her home.

And it had been fine. Well, at least until I walked back out through the double doors, when it was all I could do not to burst into tears, run back inside for a cuddle and have them both do what they always did whenever life got tough: say 'Don't worry love, it will all be okay.'

It had been seeing Dad in the hospital bed that had been the worst. Never a big man – it's from him that I get my five-foot-nothing stature – now he looked painfully small. Not frail, exactly, but definitely diminished. Weakened, as you'd expect in a man in his seventies who's been struggling with an illness for a long time.

Stop it, I told myself sternly, blowing my nose. *Get into the car, take yourself home, go and see your daughter, drink coffee, but most of all stop it. He'll be fine.*

And I had very nearly talked myself into believing he would too, except perhaps not as completely as I'd kidded myself I had, because when my mobile phone rang, just as I was coming off the dual carriageway, my first thought was *Oh, God, what's happened?*

Nothing, you stupid mare, I told myself as I took the first left turn and found a safe place to pull in. He'd barely even have had his bloods taken yet, would he? So perhaps it was Mum, with some last-minute anxiety-reducing request or other – like spare hankies or Dad's second best set of pyjamas or the current week's copy of *The People's Friend*.

But it wasn't Mum, and I found myself smiling as I read the display; it was a missed call from my fostering link worker, John Fulshaw. We'd not spoken for a while, as I'd been having a bit of downtime from fostering; we'd come out of a long placement, which had finished the previous summer, and with my daughter Riley pregnant, and Dad having been so poorly, we'd made a decision as a family to take a bit of a break. We'd only done a little respite care since.

But now it was late May – almost a year since our last child, Emma, had left us, and with Riley's daughter Marley Mae having arrived safely in April, and Dad finally getting his date for surgery, I'd already spoken to my husband Mike about suggesting to John that, come summer, we'd be back in the game.

I touched the call button, thinking how mad it was he should call at that moment. What was he, psychic or something?

Possibly. 'Ah, Casey!' he greeted me, as if I'd just returned from Mars. 'Thanks so much for getting back to me so quickly. I was worried you were on holiday –'

I laughed. 'Chance would be a fine thing, John.'

'Good,' he said. '*Good*. Well, not in that sense, of course, but good that you're around. Are you free?'

'Well, Mike and I were only recently saying …'

'No, no. *Now*. I meant "now" as in are you free right this minute? Only we have a bit of a situation.'

'Well, I was just heading home, actually.' I explained about Dad.

'Oh, I'm sorry, Casey – this really isn't a good time for you, is it? No, look, sorry – I'll have to see if I can rustle up someone else.'

He sounded crestfallen. 'No, no, John, go on. Tell me. What *is* the situation?'

'Really, Casey? You really want to know?'

'*Really*,' I confirmed, conscious of the new tone in his voice, which, after our many years of association, I had already analysed as the verbal equivalent of him crossing both his fingers and his toes. 'John, if I can help at all, I will. You know that. And to be honest, this *is* a good time because it'll take my mind off things – I'd only be pacing up and down, fretting about Dad, wouldn't I? So, go on – what is the situation?'

'I'm at the police station,' he told me.

'The police station? So that's what it is, is it? You want me to come and pay your bail?'

'A get out of jail free card might be helpful,' he mused. 'But not for me. For a boy who's here with me, name of Tyler. Eleven. Stabbed his stepmother. Nowhere to go.'

'Oh, dear,' I said, my brain already cranking into action. 'That doesn't sound too good.'

'No, it doesn't, does it? And it isn't, hence the social worker getting me down here. He's already been charged and processed and now they want shot. Only trouble is, to where?'

'So you need respite?'

'No. Well, I mean, yes, if needs be – someone's on to that currently – but we mostly need you and Mike to take him on, because this is right up your street. I don't think he's the sort of lad we can just place, ahem, anywhere. But … look, you know, you really can say no to this, Casey, if you have a lot going on in your life right now …'

'He's that bad, is he?'

'I'm not going to dress it up for you. He's likely to be challenging, so …'

So that was precisely why he had called me. As opposed to someone else. 'So shall I come down there?' I said.

'You *sure*?'

I laughed. 'I'm not sure about anything right now, John. And even if I was, I'd obviously have to speak to Mike first. And there's no way I could take him now this very minute because I obviously need to know my dad's safely out of surgery first.'

'Oh, yes, of course,' John said. 'Not a problem at all. I completely understand.'

'But in principle … Well, there's no harm in me meeting the lad, is there?'

Well, yes, actually, there was, I thought to myself as I started the engine and pulled out into the road again, police station-bound. I knew how my mind worked and it was already working overtime. An 11-year-old boy, a step-mother, nowhere to go. I was drawn like a moth to a flame.

By the time I'd got to the police station, parked and made myself known to the desk sergeant, my mood had lifted considerably. Yes, Dad was still under the knife and it *was* major surgery, but he was also fit as a flea and it was a straightforward operation. And I trusted what we'd been told – that he'd be fine.

I plonked myself down on one of the two scuffed chairs in the reception area and pulled out my phone to text Riley and let her know I'd been held up. *And by what?* I wondered.

What sort of kid was John going to introduce me to? A challenging one, definitely, because John had already spelled that out. A kid who'd be difficult to handle. As, of course, he would be, since that was the sort of child Mike and I had been trained to foster. Oh, we'd had the odd sweet, biddable child here and there – and one or two who, notably, had been absolute angels – but that wasn't our real remit. We were specialist foster carers, and our job was to take on kids who'd run out of their nine lives – certainly those who were deemed too difficult for there to be much hope of a long-term foster home as things stood, usually because of the emotional damage they had suffered in their short lives and the nightmare behaviours they displayed as a consequence. Our job was therefore to put them on an intense behaviour management programme, so they could face up to their demons, learn to control their emotions better and, hopefully, build self-esteem. It was through this, ultimately, that they would become more 'fosterable' and, in the long term, better able to cope with life.

We'd been doing it for a few years now – '*fostering the unfosterable*' as our fostering agency's strapline had it – and though we'd seen a lot in that time, much of it saddening and deeply shocking, I was always prepared to be surprised anew. So, what sort of child would this boy be, I wondered?

A very angry one, it turned out. 'Brace yourself,' John warned, once he'd come out to find me and take me through to the interview room where they were still keeping him. 'To paraphrase that advert, he's a bit of an animal.'

He also fleshed out a little of the background for me before we went in. Tyler had apparently brandished the knife – a regular carving one – during a heated argument with his stepmother and proceeded to threaten to kill her. She'd tried to get it from him, apparently telling him she'd batter him with it just as soon as she had disarmed him, which made him thrash about all the more and, according to him anyway, that was how he accidentally stabbed her in the arm.

'Though her story is different, of course,' John said. 'According to her, he most definitely didn't do it accidentally, and she's definitely going to be pressing charges.'

'And is she badly hurt?' I asked.

'No,' John said. 'Thank goodness. Just a flesh wound, which the paramedics cleaned up before taking her to hospital. Just a couple of butterfly stitches in it now, or so I'm told.'

'So she went off to hospital and he was brought here by the police?'

John nodded. 'And she's saying that's it, basically. She won't have him in the house again. No way, no how.'

'Is there a dad?'

'Yes there is, and he's apparently of the same mind. There's also a half-brother. Bit younger. The stepmother's boy.'

So there was a situation right there, I thought. We exchanged a look. Obviously John had had the same one.

Deciding to take on a new child should be a carefully thought out business. As a foster carer, you are opening not just yourself but your family and your home up to a stranger. A diminutive stranger, obviously – not a serial killer, or anything – but still a stranger about whom you start off knowing almost nothing, and what little you do know is often subjective. In this case, was the stabbing accidental or not? Without a witness, who were we supposed to believe?

So the normal course of events would usually be a multi-stage affair: an initial meeting, and, if that went okay, a formal pre-placement meeting, which would be attended by the potential foster parents, the link worker, the child in question's social worker and, of course, the child themselves. Only then, assuming all parties felt comfortable with the arrangements, would the child move in and the relationship become official.

In practice, in my case, it rarely worked that way. Yes, in most cases, the steps happened, but rarely in the right order, and the truth was that, though I didn't generally say so, I usually made up my mind about a child within minutes, not to say seconds, of making their acquaintance. And, so far, even when every warning bell had been clanging in my ears, I'd come up with the same decision. Yes.

Tyler was a beautiful boy. Inky hair flopping over deep brown and densely lashed eyes, clear olive skin, lean, sinewy build. Romany blood, I wondered? Greek? Perhaps Italian? Whatever his bloodline, he would be a heartbreaker when he was older, I decided. Might even be breaking hearts already. He was wearing a crumpled black T-shirt, low-slung combat trousers (ripped) and a pair of no doubt fashionable but very elderly trainers, all of which should have made him look like any other scruff-bag 11-year-old, but seemed to hang on his wiry frame almost stylishly.

Though there was nothing remotely stylish or, indeed, romantic about what was coming out of his mouth. 'Get your fucking hands off me!' he was railing, as John and I entered the interview room. 'I don't *wanna* fucking sit down, okay?!'

'Sit *down*!' the policeman closest to him barked, pressing him bodily back into the wooden chair on which he'd previously been sitting for his interview. He was one of three in the room, two of whom were obviously policemen – though only one was in uniform – with the third being the social worker, whose face I vaguely recognised, probably from a training session or social service gathering of some sort. He was middle-aged, slightly sweaty and looking harried.

'Ah, John,' said the nearer officer, who identified himself as PC Matlock and ushered us into the room. He closed the door firmly behind him. 'And you'll be Mrs Watson?'

I nodded. 'Casey,' I said, shaking the hand he extended.

I was about to add 'Pleased to meet you,' but the boy at the epicentre of this small earthquake beat me to it. 'An' who the fuck is she?' he yelled, springing up from the chair again, causing it to crash back onto the floor.

'Show some respect, lad!' the same policeman snapped, as Tyler glared at me and John. 'And pick that bloody chair up, as well!' But this only seemed to inflame their young charge even further; instead of picking it up he decided to use it as a football, kicking it hard enough to send it skittering across the floor.

The social worker flinched. 'Tyler, *stop* it!' he entreated. '*Behave* yourself! You are just making things worse for yourself, now, aren't you?'

To which accurate observation Tyler duly responded – by kicking the chair a second time. And then, as if pleased with the effect he was having, he drew his leg back and kicked it a third time for good measure.

The as yet unnamed policeman – this was clearly no time for introductions, much less an exchange of pleasantries – snatched the chair up. Then in one reckless action, narrowly missing the social worker, he swung it round and righted it back beside the interview table.

'That is *enough*!' he bellowed, grabbing the boy's arm and yanking him towards him, but for an 11-year-old Tyler seemed blessed with an impressive amount of strength, and had soon twisted out of his grasp. He was also still kicking out – though aiming for shins now, rather than chair legs – and with a quick 'Excuse me' PC Matlock went round both me and the table, in order to help his colleague restrain their captive raging bull sufficiently that he could be guided back into place.

'Fuck you!' Tyler yelled to the first one, as he was pressed back yet again onto the chair. 'And fuck you an' all,' he added to the other policeman. Then, as even John stepped in to try and help the social worker contain him, he used a string of words I'd not heard in a child that age in a long time, finishing with a spit, which again only narrowly missed the social worker, and a heartfelt 'And fuck you, Mr Burns!'

My response to all this was, to be fair, a bit eccentric. Yes, I was well aware that it was a very serious matter, but there was something so 'Keystone Cops' about it all, too – what with the two police officers darting back and forth trying to chase him round the table, while the social worker flapped his hands so ineffectually – that, without consciously realising it, much less wanting to do it, I found myself laughing out loud.

If I was surprised by what had come out of my mouth (where on earth *had* that come from?) the effect on Tyler was little short of electrifying. I didn't know what had made me suddenly feel the urge to giggle – perhaps the release of all that stress with Dad's op? I didn't know – but it certainly seemed to do the trick.

Because so transfixed was Tyler by this deranged woman they'd brought in to meet him that he stopped thrashing around and let them put him back on his chair. 'Who the fuck is *she*?' he said again.

Robert De Niro, I thought. Yes, he was like a very young Robert De Niro. That was why he'd put me in mind of a raging bull. Though right now this child put me in mind of another character too. A fictional one. I just couldn't seem to help it.

'I'm sorry,' I said, trying not to grin *too* much, and make him cross again. 'I'm Casey, by the way. But you know, you just reminded me so much of Bart Simpson for a minute there. You know, when you said "Fuck you, Mr Burns!" Sorry,' I said again. 'It just made me laugh.'

I glanced at the two policemen then, who, along with the hapless social worker, were looking at me with expressions of incredulity. 'Sorry,' I mumbled a third time, 'I don't know why I did that.'

Casey Watson

Tyler by this time was staring up at me intently. 'Yeah, that's because he's a knobhead,' he observed, matter of factly.

'So!' said John. 'Where shall we start?'

Chapter 2

In the end we started, as one usually does (and we hadn't been able to as yet), with a round of introductions. I learned that the colleague of PC Matlock's was a rather stressed-looking PC Harper, and that the social worker with the unfortunate name of Mr Burns was actually a duty social worker, called in to manage the emergency as best he could because Tyler's regular social worker had gone on maternity leave. And, finally, they learned who I was and what I was there for, which was not really news to the adults in the room, obviously, but caused some consternation in Tyler. While the rest of us arranged chairs in a crude semi-circle around the table, he donned the parka-style jacket that had been attached to a wall hook and pulled the hood forwards to try and hide his face. He also pushed his chair back so he wasn't part of the group. But he was watching me intently, even so.

'So, moving on. The situation with Jenny,' John said, referring to his tatty notepad, 'is that she's been involved with the family for just over a year now.' He turned to me. 'And I'll let you have a copy of her notes in due course, Casey,' he added, 'but in the meantime Will Fisher is going to take over the case.'

I nodded. Another social worker whose name was familiar, though I wasn't actually sure I'd ever met him. 'Okay,' I said, looking at Tyler and smiling. But as soon as we made eye contact, he put his head down.

'So it's really just a matter of finding a home for young master Broughton here,' PC Matlock added, again, mostly to me. 'As things stand at the moment, the parents can't take him back.'

I noticed his diplomatic use of the word 'can't', rather than 'won't', which, from what John had already told me, was obviously the truth of it.

'She's *not my fucking parent*!' Tyler yelled from his seat in the back row. 'Never was and never will be! She's a fucking witch who's always hated me!'

Mr Burns swivelled in his seat. 'All right, son. Calm down while we talk, please,' he said.

Oops, I immediately thought, given Tyler's previous comment. *Don't think I would have said that.* And I was right.

'An' I'm not your fucking son, neither, dick brain!' he snapped.

And off we went again. Ding, ding. Round two. Fortunately, by this time Tyler seemed to have run out of energy for physically railing against his captors, but over the next 20 minutes or so, while we continued to talk details, he peppered every contentious comment with his pithy take on things. So though I learned little more about the background (understandably, because there was only so much that could be discussed in front of him) one thing I did learn – and mostly via observation – was that this was a very angry, intensely troubled boy.

Mostly we were waiting, though – for a phone call to come through confirming that they had indeed found respite care for the next few days. And a knock on the door finally confirmed that perhaps it had.

'All sorted,' said the receptionist who'd been on the desk when I'd arrived. 'Couple called Smith. Very nice. Said they're happy to have Tyler – though only for a couple of days,' she added, frowning slightly, 'because they're off on their summer holiday next week. I told them to come straight down. That okay?'

'Yes, indeed,' John said, nodding. 'Perfect. Thanks very much. Good, so at least we have that bit sorted out.' He turned to me, then. 'So, Casey,' he added, looking at me with a familiar 'Well?' sort of expression, 'any chance I can put you on the spot?'

I looked over at Tyler, who, like John, had been watching my reaction, and, again, lowered his head when he caught my eye.

'Hey, Bart Simpson,' I said, forcing him to respond and meet my gaze again, 'how do you fancy coming to stay with me for a while? I'll have to speak to my husband – he's called Mike, by the way – but I'm sure he'd love to have another boy around the house. So. How about it?'

Tyler had shrunk so far into his hood by this time that he looked like he was peeping out from behind a shrubbery. 'Don't care if I do, don't care if I don't,' he said, seeming suddenly far less cocky than he had been up to now. My heart went out to him. He was 11 and he was sitting in an interview room in a police station, he was being discussed by strangers and, most of all, he wasn't going home. Didn't matter how much of a witch he had his stepmother pegged as, he *wasn't going home*. And now the adrenalin had gone, it looked like that fact was beginning to sink in. No wonder he looked like he'd had the stuffing knocked out of him.

I smiled at him again, and smiled at John. 'I'll take that as a yes, then,' I said. 'Give me a call later then, John, yes? I'm sure we can sort something out.'

'Thanks, Casey,' John said, running his hand through his hair. He patted my arm then – a familiar unspoken gesture. I knew it meant he'd been all out of options and was grateful.

'Right, then,' I said, rising from my chair. 'I'll be off, then. See you soon, Tyler, yeah?' I added, moving towards the door again. There was no response but as I turned before going through the doorway the movement of his hood told me he was watching me go.

And what was he thinking? I wondered. About his 'witch' of a stepmother? And about me? Something about frying pans and fires? I would certainly figure. I did have long black hair, after all.

'Erm, so what happened to the "Oh, it's great having all this time to spend with the grandkids" malarkey?' Mike wanted to know four short hours later, after I'd recounted the details of my strange day.

Strange, but also curiously uplifting, all things considered. Because by now, it had to be said, I was buzzing. Dad had come round and was doing great, apparently, Mum had stopped worrying and was looking after him (well, getting under the nurses' feet, more likely, bless her) and the prospect of taking on the lad I'd met earlier had gone from being a possibility to a probability to a cast iron certainty – well, in my head, at least. I still had to convince Mike.

Who was still on the same track. 'And what happened to the "Let's take a few months out from fostering" for that matter? You have a very short memory, my dear ...'

It was true. I had said all of that. And when I'd said it, I'd truly meant it. But the very fact that Mike was teasing me about it was a Very Good Sign Indeed. If he'd been set against it, he wouldn't be teasing. He'd be frowning. As it was I knew I wouldn't have to work too hard to convince him.

'Oh, shut up!' I said, throwing a cushion in his general direction for good measure. 'And, anyway, it's been almost a year now. If we leave it much longer we'll probably have to do retraining. And we don't want to have to go through the faff of all that, do we?'

I didn't actually know if we would have to retrain – but it seemed a fair bet we would in some way, shape or form. At the very least in some aspect of health and safety. You couldn't turn around for new health and safety initiatives, after all, could you? So it was less 'little white lie' and more 'overemphasising the negative' because I knew it was something that would get him. And I'd been right – a look of horror began spreading across his face. Big and assertive and managerial as he was, my husband was cringingly shy when it came to things involving group participation. And that was something the fostering training process had had in spade loads: lots of role play with fellow trainees and lots of speaking in public. It would be his worst nightmare to have to do it all again.

He dried his hands – he'd been just finishing off the last of the drying up – and now came to join me on the sofa.

'Okay, so what's this kid like, then?' he asked. 'The real, unvarnished truth, mind. And when were you thinking of him moving in?'

I took a moment to try and think how best to convey my first impressions, and though I could think of lots of ways to couch 'stabbed his stepmum' in such a manner that it would sugar the pill slightly, I realised it was probably best to prepare for the worst and then work upwards. 'I'm not going to lie to you, love,' I said. 'He looks like he might be a proper little handful, to be honest. He swears like a trooper and had a bit of a temper on him, too. One that …' To say or not to say? Yes, say, Casey. 'Well, remember when Justin first came to us?'

Mike nodded. Slowly. 'Oh dear.'

'Well, yes, you say that,' I countered, turning to face him on the sofa and swinging my legs up beneath me. 'I mean, he turned out to be such a lovely kid, didn't he? And look at him now! Imagine if we hadn't given him that chance? And, well, was it so difficult, *really*, looking back?'

Mike gave me what my mum would call an old-fashioned look, and perhaps not without very good reason. Justin had been our first ever foster child and his horrendous background (and, boy, it had been a grim one) had caused him to not only build a wall right around him but also the mental equivalent of a roll of barbed wire – he had a tendency to lash out at anyone who tried to help him. His behaviour had been so bad that one previous carer had been moved to point out that he was 'a newspaper headline just waiting to happen' – and not one about the Queen's Jubilee.

For almost a year Justin had turned our lives upside down – and not just Mike and my lives either; the whole family had been involved, particularly our youngest, Kieron, then still in his teens. But it had worked out okay. We eventually got to the root of everything. And Justin had turned out to be like any other kid; hurting and sad and abandoned and alone, and, once he had some love and stability, he responded positively. He blossomed before our eyes, and he grew.

And Justin, fully grown now, was still in our lives, testament to the fact that love and stability had a lot to be said for it. Love and stability, in most cases, worked.

And we could offer that to *this* lad, though I sensed I didn't need to bang on about it.

'You're right, I suppose,' Mike agreed – though he might still have had half a mind on 'Pretend you're the foster dad and that Mrs Potter is this young girl who is coming on to you …' Either way, I could tell we were on. 'And if it turns out to get a bit lively, well, I suppose it keeps us on our toes, doesn't it?' he added. 'Keeps us young.'

I laughed at that, though I'd be lying if I said I wasn't nervous. 'Young' was one thing we weren't. I was 47 now and Mike was a year older. And though that didn't make us old, it did make me rational. There were lots of ways of defining the word 'lively', after all. And given the sort of kids we had tended to foster so far, I reckoned our definition probably wasn't the same as most …

Chapter 3

Because the respite carers were off on holiday within a couple of days of Tyler joining them, we didn't have much time to get organised. Which was nothing new – we were used to taking in children at short notice – but, given the length of time since our last stint of fostering, 'getting organised' this time wasn't just a case of making a bed up; it involved making a bed visible in the first place. It didn't matter how many times I pointed out the meaning of the term 'spare' room, we were all guilty (even our grown-up kids who No Longer Lived With Us) of using the ones we had – three of them now, all told – as a free branch of Safestore.

But I was happy enough to roll my sleeves up and get stuck in, not only because it gave me something physical to do – always a great stress-buster – but also because I felt the familiar buzz of excitement that always accompanied saying yes to a new child. It was the thrill of the challenge; the anticipation of finding out what made them tick.

That this one needed a temporary loving home was obviously a given, but apart from that we knew very little else, due to Tyler's social worker being away on maternity leave. Not that John hadn't tried. He'd at least managed to establish a couple of facts.

'Or, rather, problems,' he'd corrected, when he'd popped round the day before and I'd asked him what facts he did know – over and above the parents' names, anyway, which were apparently Gareth and Alicia. 'He's been with them since he was three and there've apparently been problems pretty much since the start.'

'And before that?'

'Before that he was with his birth mother, now deceased. Died of a drug overdose. He's been with dad and stepmum ever since.'

I frowned, taking this in. So sad. So familiar. 'Overdose,' I parroted.

'Yes,' John confirmed. 'Though whether accidental or intentional, I don't as yet know. Though I will, of course, just as soon as –'

'Don't tell me. The paperwork comes through?'

He grinned wryly. 'You know the drill, Casey. But it shouldn't be too long. His new social worker's been assigned so it's just a case of him familiarising himself with the notes. We know there's an element of urgency here, too, what with the charges ...'

But I was now with that three-year-old whose mum had taken an overdose. 'Oh, the poor kid. Though I guess, being three when it happened, one blessing is that he won't much remember his mum ...'

'I imagine not,' John agreed. 'But I don't think that's the main issue. From what I've gleaned, it's the relationship with the stepmum that's key here. And it sounds like it's not without precedent. She had her own baby, didn't she? And it's a pound to a penny that she wasn't too happy to have another woman's toddler dumped on her, don't you think?'

'Certainly sounds that way,' I said, feeling saddened by the inevitability of it all. It didn't have to be that way but, in this case, it apparently was – the unwanted toddler having turned into an unloved pre-pubescent boy, who had responded in kind. And with a knife.

'Anyway, Thursday at 2 p.m. – is that going to work for you?' asked John. 'Oh, and do you think you can work some magic? You know, with school? Almost forgot to tell you – he's been excluded from his.'

I rolled my eyes. '*Now* you tell me!'

He raised his palms in supplication. 'Sorry, Casey – I only found that out myself this morning. A case of too many incidents of fighting, and too many last chances, I'm afraid.'

As it was, I knew I probably wouldn't have too much trouble persuading the head of the local comprehensive to have Tyler, not least because before going into fostering I'd worked there myself for several years. I'd been a behaviour manager, running a unit for the most challenging and challenged kids – the bullied and the bullies, the dispossessed and the disruptive; it was the job that ultimately led to me and Mike making the decision that becoming specialist foster carers was the thing we wanted to do.

As I'd thought, it had only taken a phone call. Of course, that wasn't to say Mr Moore wouldn't regret his largesse once Tyler went there – but taking on a child that had been excluded from another school didn't tend to be something you agreed to if you didn't at least have an inkling of what you might be taking on. But that had been yesterday and school wasn't an issue till next week. Right now, I had just over a day and a half to prepare our home – not to mention our lives – for the new member of the family which, in my case, because I'm pathologically obsessed with cleaning, meant a spring clean (my second) and a bit of a clear-out.

Which, as Mike was at work, and Riley was much too busy with her own little addition, meant enlisting my son Kieron to give me a hand.

Kieron was working too – he had recently completed an NVQ and was now a part-time teaching assistant at the local primary school, as well as coaching a youth football team in his spare time – but, as his hours were flexible, I knew he wouldn't mind coming round to give me a hand, not least because 'organisation' was his middle name.

Kieron has what used to be called Asperger's. These days they'd tend to say he has a mild ASD, or autism spectrum disorder, but back then (he was diagnosed while still in primary school) it was known as Asperger's syndrome, and manifested itself as an array of behaviours, such as having some difficulty relating to peers, disliking change (it did and still does make him anxious) and liking all his belongings to be just so – or woe betide whoever messed them up. He was also a bit of a fact-fiend: the archetypal child who could always tell you which actor was in which

movie and who kept his CDs ad DVDs in perfect alpha-
betical order.

And just as Kieron's Asperger's taught me and Mike so
much that we were able to use once we started fostering, so
I was able to teach Kieron all sorts of things about cleaning
houses, not to mention recruit him to help me willingly at
times such as these.

We were now surveying the bedrooms we'd just cleared
out between us, deciding which would be the best for Tyler
to go in. I had three spare rooms since no one was currently
living with us: the pink and blue ones, which I'd had the
foresight to decorate thus, to cover both fostering bases,
plus one that we'd decorated neutrally with a plan to keep
it for visiting relatives. Though, as it had worked out, it had
been pressed into service for a foster child or two as well;
most notably when we looked after a more profoundly
autistic boy, Georgie, who couldn't cope with being in
either a pink *or* a blue room. As with everything to do with
fostering, we lived and learned.

But the furniture in there was old and fusty – including
the family heirloom wardrobe. Had I been 11 it wasn't the
room I'd have chosen, to be sure. 'So the blue room makes
sense,' I said to Kieron, 'because that's half the job done
already. But how do I dress it up? What do 11-year-old
boys currently like?'

It wasn't as much of a no-brainer question as it might
have seemed. Fashions changed so quickly where kids were
concerned, and though I could give you chapter and verse
on my little grandsons I had no idea what was currently 'in'
with older boys.

'How should I know?' said Kieron, shrugging. 'I'm not the oracle, Mum! Probably football, but then again, possibly not. Some of the kids on my team like playing it but are less into watching it – some are much more into computer games ...'

'But *which* computer games?'

'How should I know?' he said, laughing. 'Actually, I *do* know. Super Mario – he'll probably like Super Mario *anything* – Rayman, Minecraft ... pretty much anything like that ... But, really, you won't know till you get to know him, will you?'

'So how am I supposed to sort the bloody room out for him, then?'

Kieron gave me an old-fashioned look. 'Mum, he's not been beamed down from Mars, has he? Won't he already *have* stuff? You said he was coming from a family home, didn't you? Not some poorhouse out of Dickens.'

'I know ... oh, I just should have asked him what he liked, shouldn't I?'

'Mother,' said my son firmly, 'the room is just *fine*. There's a TV, a DVD player – what more's he going to need? And I'm sure he'll tell you if there's anything he needs desperately. You're so funny. You know what this is, don't you? Just anxiety.' He pulled his sweatshirt sleeves back down in an unambiguous gesture. It said 'We're done, so stop your flapping,' so I did.

Even so, I couldn't resist popping down to a couple of nearby charity shops the following morning, just to make the room look a little more lived in. A couple of football annuals, some superhero books, a brace of boyish-looking jigsaws and a construction set, even if I did chastise myself mentally as I did so. *How* many bloody times had I done this already?

In an ideal world, it would only have been once or twice, with each new child only requiring a bit of a top-up. That was always the plan – to keep a stock of toys and so on (we could ill afford to keep buying new stuff, after all) so that I would have things that would suit any child. It never happened like that, though. Whenever a child left us, I'd always pile everything up and give it to them to ensure they always had stuff they could call their own wherever they were moving on to next. And it wasn't just me being wet, either. Once you've had children show up on your doorstep with nothing but the clothes on their back – literally, not a single thing to call their own – it's not an image you can easily forget.

I threw in a new duvet set as well – well, they were on special offer in the supermarket – and by the time 2 p.m. Thursday rolled around, I was happy. All that remained was my ceremonial flick-around with the duster – such an ingrained tradition that Mike was considering getting me a special gold ceremonial pinny in which to do it. He'd taken a few hours off work in order that we could both welcome Tyler and was hovering as per usual, either waiting for me to give him the next 'essential' job to do, or challenging me to dare to – I was never quite sure which.

'Mike, go to the window,' I told him. 'Keep an eye out and yell as soon as you see the car, okay? I want to have the kettle boiled ready.' I glanced at the dining-room table. 'Do you think I've put out enough biscuits?'

He guffawed. He actually guffawed. 'Calm down, woman!' he said, same as he said every time. 'You're acting as if we've never done this before. Everything is perfect. The house is completely spotless … Ah – well, apart from those five biscuit crumbs I dropped on the table when I pinched one, of course.'

I glared at him, half-knowing he was winding me up but unable to resist looking at the table even so. 'Pig!' I said. 'It's not funny, and besides, Mr Clever Clogs, it's a long time since we've done this – nearly two years!'

But he wasn't listening, he was looking, and now he flapped a hand. 'Uh, oh,' he said, letting the curtain go. 'Time for kettle duty I think, Case. Looks like they're here.'

Tyler looked no different than he had the first time I'd met him. Sullen and grumpy and reluctant to engage. What was going through his mind, I wondered, as Mike held out a hand for him to shake. This was a massive upheaval in his young life, having to move in with us. How did he feel about it? Was it a relief to be away from his apparently hated stepmother? Was he anxious? Was he bewildered? Was he scared?

Probably all of the above, I thought, even if the expression on his face was a visual depiction of 'Yeah, whatever'.

'Hi, Tyler!' I said brightly, extending an arm so I could usher him in. 'Nice to see you again. D'you want to choose a seat at the table? And help yourself to juice and biscuits, of course. I didn't know which ones you liked so I put out the ones *I* like. That way,' I quipped, 'if you don't like them, there'll be all the more for me.'

He plonked himself down and looked at me as if I was mad.

'There you go, lad,' Mike said, having pulled out the seat Tyler had just sat on. He then sat down beside him. 'Casey'll be lucky. Jammie Dodgers and Jaffa Cakes are my favourites too –' he took one to illustrate – 'Go on, help yourself,' he urged, 'or I'll scoff down the lot.'

Tyler took the glass of juice John had by now poured for him, but refused Mike's offer with a head shake. 'I only like chocolate-chip ones,' he said pointedly.

I leapt up again, having only just parked my backside. This was fine. If he was testing our mettle then so be it. If not, then so be it, too. 'Well,' I said, 'it just so happens that I have some of those as well. They're our son Kieron's favourite. Shall I go and get some?'

Tyler shook his head. 'Nah,' he said. 'I'm not hungry.'

Okay, I thought. If that's how he wants to play it, that's fine. 'Okay,' I said, 'not to worry. It'll be teatime soon anyway. Perhaps you'll have worked up an appetite by then.'

Or, indeed, a sentence, because as the meeting got under way I had the same sense as I had had in the police station that Tyler was happy zoning out and letting people talk about him, rather than to him. It was perhaps a typical response for a boy of his age, particularly when in the company of strangers, but I wondered if it was also something he was used to doing at home anyway. Though he was listening intently (that was obvious) he showed no inclination to have an input – and even when invited to contribute directly, it was like pulling teeth. So we went

Caey Waton

through all the usual details, the care plan and the various items of paperwork (we had to be given 'parental' responsibility for things like GP and dental appointments) while Tyler just sat there, jacket on, hood down only grudgingly (following John's directive about hoods at the table), present yet absent, being talked over. So I was glad when John – presumably thinking the same thought that I was – asked Mike if he'd mind giving Tyler the usual tour.

'Would you mind showing him his new room and so on, Mike,' he asked him, 'while Casey and I go through the last of the signatures? Then we'll get Tyler's stuff out of the car so we can get him installed properly.'

Mike looked relieved to be doing something. He sprang into action, rising from his seat and giving Tyler a gentle nudge. 'Come on then, mate,' he said. 'Let's go and take a look at where you'll be laying your head down for a bit, shall we?'

To which Tyler responded by flicking his hood back up, getting up, shoving his hands into his tracksuit bottom pockets and following Mike, without a word, out of the room.

'And if I know Casey,' I heard Mike say as they headed up the stairs, 'you might have to move some clutter to make some room for all your bits and bobs.'

I didn't hear Tyler's reply.

'Well,' said John, taking off his reading glasses and running a hand though his hair, 'as meetings go, that one felt a little pointless, didn't it? Though if it's any consolation, he's been giving the respite carers a pretty tough time of it, so it's

30

nothing personal.' He grinned. 'In fact, the last thing they said to me was that if they hadn't already planned their holiday, they would have done so by now.'

I smiled. 'That bad, eh?' I helped myself to one of the Jaffa Cakes. 'Anyway, I didn't think that – it's hardly surprising he's off with us, is it? What with the court case and everything. Assuming that's still happening. Is it?'

'I'm afraid it looks like it,' John said. 'It's the knife. If there hadn't been the knife involved, he might have got away with a stern telling off, particularly given his age, but as it stands, and with the way the stepmother seems so determined to make him pay, then, yes, court seems inevitable. You'll probably be asked to speak up for him, too, as no doubt you already know. Well, if that proves possible.' He gave me a wry smile.

'Optimism, John, okay? That's the thing here. And, well, there you go,' I added. 'He's probably bricking it, wondering what the hell is going to become of him. Don't worry, John. We'll get him on track. Warm him up. Make him see we're on his side. One day at a time, eh? More coffee?'

John accepted a second cup and while Mike took his time upstairs (he knew the drill) caught me up on a couple of things that he hadn't mentioned in front of Tyler, including some more specific details surrounding his exclusion; Tyler's aggressive streak was, it seemed, a thick one. And that wasn't the only reason John was pleased to hear I'd persuaded the head of the local comp to take him in. He'd also managed to glean that because the family had recently moved house the younger brother, Grant, was now in the comp's catchment area – he was currently in year six of one of their feeder primaries, which meant, in theory, that come September, assuming Tyler was still with us, the boys would at least be reunited in school.

'It's definitely looking that serious, then?' I asked him. 'No family reconciliation looking likely?'

'You can never say never,' John said, 'but we're working on the worst case scenario. From what they're saying at the moment, this is very much a last straw situation – who knows what the dad would do if left to his own devices, but as of now their position's clear – they are washing their hands of him. This isn't his first violent outburst at home, apparently – far from it. And, given what we know of his behaviour in school, we have to believe the family are telling the truth. They clearly don't have a clue what to do with him any more.'

At the age of just 11. It was heartbreaking. How had it come to that? It wasn't even as if he was a particularly big, strong boy, either. How had he come to be an object of such fear?

'So he's going on the programme with us?' I asked, mentally rolling my sleeves up. 'Doing all the usual points and levels?'

'Definitely,' John said. 'Starting asap.'

The 'programme' was what our kind of fostering was mostly based on. When a child first arrived they would be on a regime of very basic privileges, including TV time, computer time and time playing out with friends. In order to do any of those things, a child would have to 'buy' the time they needed, using the points that they accumulated each day. To earn those points, they would be expected to do a number of set tasks, each of which carried a points value, and with which they could 'buy' things for the following day. The programme was tailored to each individual child and the tasks would differ according to their needs. We had siblings once, for example, who'd come from an extremely neglectful background and had no idea about personal hygiene. They would therefore go to the toilet almost anywhere in the house, then, after wiping themselves with their bare hands, smear excrement on the walls. Their programme therefore reflected this, being loaded with items such as 'Do not poo or wee anywhere other than the toilet – 30 points' and 'Wash hands and face and brush teeth every morning and before bed – 30 points', and so on. In Tyler's case these basic life-skills were givens (we hoped) so his points would be geared mostly to good behaviour.

'Okay,' I said to John now, hearing Mike and Tyler coming back downstairs. 'But I think "asap" should mean Monday. Let's let the dust settle. See what the next couple of days throw up first. Give us a chance to get to know him a little better first, at least.'

'Okay,' said John, beginning to gather his papers up. 'Sounds good. And I think it's time I got out of your hair. Short and sweet, but I think our little chap has had enough of authority, don't you?' He smiled. 'Don't they all? Anyway, email me your proposed programme as soon as you have it and I'll pass it on to the powers that be for the official sanction. Oh, and fix something up with Will Fisher – have him come round and meet you, fill you in a bit more, just as soon as he's on top of things in the office, not to

Casey Watson

mention the case. He's taken over several from Jenny, so it might be a week or so yet, unless you feel a pressing need to have him round here sooner?'

I shook my head. Mike and I were well used to going in blind. Yes, I was keen to hear more about Tyler's background – that could only be helpful. But, unless there was some major crisis that required the social worker's input, there was no desperate rush.

'Well,' Mike said, coming back in. 'Tyler likes his room, don't you, Tyler? And we've more or less worked out where all his stuff is going to go.' He smiled across at Tyler, who was standing in the doorway, hood still up, chewing his nails. Mike grinned at him. 'Cat got your tongue again, lad?'

And for his cheerfulness and patience he was amply rewarded – by an even more spectacular scowl than his previous ones.

Ouch, I thought, mirroring John's raised eyebrows. Sleeves definitely up, then. This was going to be fun.

Chapter 4

The next couple of days were spent establishing ground rules. Though we weren't planning on starting Tyler on the behaviour management programme till the following Monday, we still needed to put some basic boundaries in place about what was and what wasn't acceptable. After all, we knew virtually nothing about him – and what we did know didn't put him in the best light, all told, since it mostly involved a knife and a school exclusion.

And the need for boundaries became clear before John had even left us; while he was still being kind, and helping bring his young charge's things in, in fact.

'Careful, you dickhead!' he'd yelled at John, when the football annual he'd had wedged under his arm had accidentally fallen on the grass. He'd followed that gem up with an equally friendly explanation that 'My mate Cameron nicked that for me!'

While John had chastised Tyler for his language – not to mention his ingratitude – I made a mental note of the name Cameron, for future reference.

I would soon learn who Cameron was, in any case, as Tyler's response was to whine that it was the only thing he had to remind him of his best friend, upon which John (who obviously already knew) pointed out that, as Cameron only lived five minutes away from where we did, it was hardly as if they were at opposite ends of the world.

I took all this in as well, filing it in my brain automatically. And I was soon to learn more. Cameron, it seemed, was both Tyler's friend and his hero – he talked about him so much that it soon became obvious that he was perhaps the most important role-model in his life. Though not necessarily of the positive kind – he was a 15-year-old boy Tyler had known since he'd moved in with his dad. And, from what I could glean, he was a bit of a neglected, latch-key kid – the only child of a single mum who was out all the time (for what reason Tyler knew not, but apparently not work), leaving her son to roam the estate where they lived. From what Tyler told me – of how he sofa-surfed, cadged rides and went to friends' houses for food – I was surprised to learn that, as far as Tyler knew, anyway, he'd never been taken into care himself.

But it was the child in *our* care who preoccupied me most, not least because, despite Kieron's confidence, given Tyler's home background, he'd come with so little to call his own. He didn't even have a case or holdall – just a green recycling bag filled with clothing, and a cardboard box full of old games and toys. There was the precious annual (separate only because he'd apparently been reading it on the journey), some tatty Marvel comics and figurines, a well-worn football and a torn photograph – of him as a baby, he said – that had been taped back together, plus, of course, the ubiquitous mobile phone. Needless to say, it didn't take much time to find a place for everything, so it wasn't long – after a longer tour around the house and garden – before we got our second taste of Tyler's short temper.

We'd finally got him to remove his hoodie, at least, and I think that was only because it was such a warm day, and he had wandered into the front room to watch some TV, while I got started cooking our tea. I was making sausages and mash – a family favourite – and had just finished peeling the potatoes when I heard the commotion from the living room. Taking off my apron and drying my hands, I walked through to see what was going on. Tyler was standing by the window, clutching the remote control, his face angry and contorted. Mike was on his feet too, and was holding out his hand.

'Just pass it back to me, Tyler,' he was saying. 'It's a simple enough request. We don't speak to each other like that in this house.'

'And I said fuck off!' Tyler yelled, glaring at poor Mike. 'All I wanted to do was see if my cartoons were on. And *that's* a simple enough 'quest an' all!'

'Tyler, you didn't make a *request*,' Mike answered levelly. 'You just took the remote from beside me and changed the channel, without saying *anything*. I was watching something – which you could see – but I would have happily turned it over if you'd asked me.'

I went to join Mike. 'Tyler, give Mike the remote back, please,' I asked him nicely. 'It's almost tea time so there's no time for cartoons just yet anyway, and, like Mike said, we won't have that kind of language in this house.'

Tyler switched his glare to me then, and threw the remote onto the sofa, just missing Mike as it landed. 'I knew this place would be shit!' he said with a harsh and scornful laugh. 'I won't stay,' he said. 'I told that John. I'm not going to stay in this shit-hole!' He then marched across the room, swerving past us.

I'd have probably let him go, but Mike stepped out to stop him. 'Not so fast, young man,' he said. 'We're not done here.'

'Could you move, *please*?' Tyler asked him.

'In a moment,' Mike replied. 'But first of all you need to know this, Tyler. It doesn't matter where you come from or what it is you are accustomed to, but we are the adults here, okay? We are entrusted to show you the ropes and look after you properly. And that includes teaching you about good manners and how to treat others. I'm going to let this go just now because it's your first day here and it's bound to be strange for you. But I'm telling you now that we don't tolerate this kind of behaviour. Now go on, either go up to your room or go and play in the garden. Tea will be ready when Casey calls you, okay? It's up to you if you're hungry or not.'

I watched, open-mouthed, as Mike then stepped aside to let Tyler pass. Which he did, keeping it zipped as he stomped up the stairs. Mike stared after him, his expression one of intense irritation, as if he'd just hit the point when it all came flooding back – just what fostering a kid like this was actually going to entail. 'Wow,' I said, once I knew Tyler was safely out of earshot. 'That was impressive. Like riding a bike, eh? Or did you have that rehearsed?'

He shook his head, and sat back down on the sofa. 'Didn't need to,' he said, picking up the remote from where Tyler had flung it. 'You know, I actually even had my *hand* on this when he took it. Just marched up, pulled it from under my hand, and turned the telly over without so much as a bloody word! If he'd said anything at all – *anything* – I'd have given him the bloody thing without a second thought. But I'll be damned if I'm going to be spoken to like that for nothing!'

Mike was talking as if he felt he needed to justify giving Tyler a dressing down, which couldn't have been further from the truth. He'd dealt with him brilliantly, without raising his voice, or showing anger – just using quiet but firm authority. Yet I could see he was rattled about it, and that rattled me. It *had* been a long time since we'd had a child in, and an even longer time since we'd had a boy – well, if you didn't count the babies – because our last had been a teenage girl. It had been an even longer time since we'd had a boy of Tyler's age and level of anger, and I wondered if it wasn't hitting home to Mike, even as he sat there, just how much of the boundary-maintenance would naturally fall to him.

'Come help me sort the tea out?' I asked him, even though I didn't actually need any. 'Fingers crossed the message has hit home, and he'll be down for his tea, and we can start again on a more positive note. It'll sink in,' I added, as he rose to join me, his expression still very much one that said, *What have we got ourselves into here?* 'You know how it goes, love,' I reassured him. 'Sooner or later it will.'

Mike sighed heavily as he followed me through to the kitchen. 'Let's hope it's sooner then, eh?' he said, as he began gathering up the potato peelings. 'At least I can escape to work, love. You don't have that luxury.' He picked up the vegetable knife, and I knew exactly what he was thinking as he studied it. 'You might have to be braced for this sort of thing every day.'

That little incident, minor though it was, set a tone that lasted into the weekend. Tyler, perhaps understandably, didn't want to be with us. Which was not to say he wanted to be home – not with the 'witch' living there, anyway – but it didn't make him any keener on making friends with us. He'd come down to tea and seemed to enjoy it – albeit in a dogged silence – but he seemed entirely resistant to the idea of my hastily penned 'house rules'. I'd run them up that Thursday evening, as a taster of what was coming on the Monday, including such staples as no swearing, respect others in the house, bed at 8.00 p.m., lights out at 9.00 p.m.

All of them were broken within a day. And were broken several times over by the end of the following week, so by the time the next Saturday rolled around it was less a question of what rules he'd broken than casting about to find one he hadn't. Worse than that, on that Saturday – after I'd had to tell Tyler off about his bad language for what felt like the tenth time that day – Kieron called in to see us after his morning football session. He couldn't have chosen a more inopportune time.

'Afternoon!' I heard him call through the house. I was sorting the washing out in the back porch and hurried back inside. Tyler was in the living room, and this would be the first time they encountered one another. And it was a relationship I was hoping to nurture.

'Oh hi, love,' I said as I saw Tyler, who was sprawled across the sofa, eyeing up Kieron with curiosity. 'Good game? This is Tyler,' I added. 'He's into football, too, aren't you, Tyler?'

'Nice one,' said Kieron. 'Good to meet you at last, mate. What team do you support?'

Tyler looked like he might answer, but then his face changed and he shrugged. He then turned his attention back to the TV in what was unquestionably a deliberate snub. I bridled. Kieron might be 25, and he might not give a damn about the opinion of this arsey 11-year-old stranger, but I felt affronted and angry on his behalf. I knew it wouldn't bother him that much, but I also knew the way my son's mind worked – he found rudeness of any kind particularly difficult to process. Yes, he was better than he'd been as a child – the world of work had toughened him up a bit in that regard – but that was work and this was home (his family home, even if he no longer lived with us) and he shouldn't have to put up with some little tyke being rude to him within it.

'Tyler,' I said pointedly, 'Kieron was asking you a question, love. He asked you which team you supported.'

I waited, hoping to force him into continuing the conversation. I soon wished I hadn't.

'And I heard him!' he snapped back, quick as you like. 'And I told him I don't know!'

He launched himself off the sofa, then, and for a moment I thought he was going to run at me and rugby tackle me, but instead he headed straight for Kieron and the open door. 'Oh, for God's sake!' he shouted. 'Can't you people just leave me *alone*?'

'Hey!' Kieron barked. 'Less of the lip. You don't talk to my mum like that, Tyler, do you hear?'

Tyler ignored him, barging past him and stomping out of the living room, slamming the door behind him for good measure.

'What the hell?' Kieron said, shaking his head. 'Was it something I said?'

I squeezed his arm. 'No, love,' I said. 'He's been like this since he got here. Take no notice. He's on his last gasp, in any case. Me and your dad are giving him the weekend to settle down a bit and then we'll start to work on that God-awful behaviour of his. You know what it's like,' I added, picking up the remote and silencing the din from the TV. 'He's come from a really bad place, love. And he's currently "adjusting".'

Kieron grinned. 'Mum, *all* the kids you have come from a bad place. He's just – did you hear that? Was that the front door I just heard go?'

I sighed heavily. He wasn't planning on doing a runner, was he? Now, that would be a *great* start. I ran to the front window. 'Oh, it's all right,' I said. 'He's just taken his football out into the front garden. Maybe he's going to have a kick-about to calm himself down.'

'Let's hope you're right,' Kieron answered wryly. 'Let's hope he hasn't decided to try take it out on the house.'

No sooner had Kieron said that than I was reminded of one of my mum's famous sayings: *Many a true word is spoken in jest*.

The sudden thud was almighty. 'Jesus! He bloody is!' I said in amazement, watching his antics. 'He's purposely kicking the ball at the front door!'

And hard, too. Kieron joined me at the window just as the second 'hit' landed. This time, however, it wasn't the door we heard rattle. It was the unmistakable sound of breaking glass. 'What the …?' Kieron spluttered, before rushing out into the hall. I followed him, desperately hoping that it had been an unfortunate accident, but knowing, without a doubt, that it was not.

'Kieron!' I said, as he yanked the front door open, 'just stay calm, love. Let's see what he has to say for himself first.' Too late.

'I saw that!' Kieron shouted at Tyler, as I surveyed the puddle of broken glass shards that had rained down from the side panel of my front door. 'You kicked that ball at that pane of glass on purpose!'

'Did I fuck!' Tyler responded. 'You want your eyes testing! *God*,' he added, stabbing a tightly balled fist into each hip, 'see what I mean? I get the blame for *everything* in this shit-hole!'

Kieron skewered him on the end of a premier-league scowl and hoicked a thumb behind him. 'Get inside right now!' he said. 'And don't think I won't pick you up and bring you in,' he added.

At which point I decided to intervene. I didn't want the neighbours' curtains twitching at my latest drama, but nor did I want Tyler antagonising my son. 'There'll be no need to do that, love,' I said quietly to Kieron. 'Tyler, *get* in here, *now*! I *mean* it.'

But if I thought my own brand of hard talking would do the trick, I was wrong. 'Fuck off, you fat bitch!' he yelled back, leaving me stunned. *Fat*? I knew I'd put on a few pounds in the last year or so (sympathy eating for two and spending too much time with hungry grandsons), but at just under ten stone I preferred to think I was pleasantly plump – at the very worst. Cheeky little sod! But I barely had time to reply when my son barged past me and made a grab for him. 'In here! Now!' he said, gripping Tyler firmly by his right shoulder, clearly offended by the weight-slur on my behalf. And if that surprised me, I was totally gobsmacked by what happened next. The 11-year-old whirlwind whirled and, despite the difference in their heights, managed to land a punch that hit Kieron firmly on the chin. Clearly taken aback, Kieron nevertheless held on while Tyler tried to capitalise on his advantage by kicking him in the shins. If it wasn't so horrifying it would have been comical. Kieron, my six foot three beanpole of a son, was skipping around, trying to fend off kicks, punches and bites, while this little scrap of a kid gave it everything he had. And not just physically – he was giving his all vocally as well, turning the air blue with his colourful language.

'Get off me, you shitty bastard!' he screamed as Kieron held on. 'Get your fucking hands off me, you cunt!'

I was mesmerised, I think, but thoughts of the neighbours again roused me, and I plunged in to try and separate them without delay. 'Tyler!' I yelled as I grabbed him by the hoodie. 'Stop that right now and get inside, you hear me?'

It took some tugging but I eventually managed to get him away and pin both his arms to his sides. I leaned in then, and spoke quietly, close to his face. 'I swear, Tyler,' I hissed. 'I won't be telling you this again. Get in that house and go to your room. This is your last chance.'

I meant it too. Right then, I did, anyway. We'd had him a scant week and a bit, and, though it was entirely out of character, I could easily see myself calling John and telling him we'd changed our minds. It was so unlike me, but, when I considered it (coolly, as Tyler stood there and scowled at me) I realised that he hadn't done a single tiny thing that would let me warm to him.

Not that I expected him to do that consciously, of course I didn't. But with almost every kid I'd ever dealt with, I could see past that. See the tiniest chink of something through their spiky, gnarly armour, sense the pain and the need for love in their bruised souls.

And it was then – at that very moment – that finally I thought I glimpsed it. It was only fleeting; so swift that I could easily have missed it. But as he struggled from my grasp, it crossed his face. It was so subtle; just the tiniest jut of his chin, but I could read it. It said, *Go on, then. Hate me. I've given you enough ammo now, haven't I?* It was enough –

just – to remind me that he was like this for a reason. I let him go then, and he thundered up the stairs.

I was shaking a little as I followed him back inside – I was clearly unused to the adrenalin rush. 'Oh, Kieron,' I said, as he bent down to start picking up the larger glass shards, 'I'm so sorry you had to go through all that. I just can't believe it,' I called back, running into the kitchen to get the dustpan. 'I really can't, honestly. Are you okay, love?'

Kieron surprised me then, by shrugging it off, and even smiling at me. 'I'm fine,' he said. 'Mum, you forget. I deal with little tykes like that every flipping day.'

Which couldn't be true – either that, or his school had serious discipline issues – but it was still a reminder that my little boy wasn't a little boy any more and no longer quite as vulnerable.

'I know you do,' I said anyway, 'but you don't need that sort of thing when you're here, do you?'

He took the dustpan. 'I don't know,' he said. 'Probably did him good. I think he at least has my measure now, don't you?'

I looked at the broken window pane. How much was that going to cost to replace? One thing was for sure – this boy needed some swift and serious input. *So come Monday*, I thought grimly as we cleared the last of the glass, *he's going to have my bloody measure, too.*

Chapter 5

With our 'pre'-placement meeting scheduled for nine thirty (what had possessed me?) it was a mad dash just getting back from dropping Tyler off at high school, let alone making anything like the sort of domestic effort I'd have wanted to before John and Tyler's new social worker descended on me.

It was another Thursday – I could hardly believe it had been a full fortnight we'd had Tyler now – and the house felt not so much messy as 'invaded'. And not just by the enormous chart – already filling up with ticks and numbers – that now spanned the entire top door of the fridge-freezer. No, we were experiencing an advanced case of 'child-creep'. I've always been a bit OCD about cleaning – something I probably inherited from my mother – and one thing our extended period without a child staying had done was to furnish me with some pretty big rose-tinted glasses. Forget the wall-to-wall tension, the shouting and the equally noisy stony silences – how had it slipped my mind what a huge a difference in the domestic workload one 11-year-old boy could make? Particularly one who was so volatile. And life had already felt something of a whirlwind, in any case, even without the one-child tornado now residing with us. Dad was well on the mend, but I still needed to help Mum with a lot of the day-to-day domestics, and I was very conscious that Riley also had a lot on her plate, so I was trying to juggle hurricane Tyler with the twin mini-typhoons that were my grandsons. Another thing I'd forgotten was quite how many 'runs' were involved in Levi and Jackson's school, nursery and social commitments, and it was all I could do to draw breath.

I took a deep one now as I turned the car into the drive and found my eye inescapably drawn to the still taped-up glass panel at the side of my front door. And in doing so, I yet again asked myself the same question – had I been just a bit too impulsive in rushing to take Tyler on? Was this really the best time in our lives to be behaviour-managing a boy who had such extreme anger? Had I been selfish in even considering it? And not just in terms of my own commitments, either. Was it really fair on the rest of the family? This was my absolute last chance to pull out, and I knew it.

I climbed out of the car and headed indoors to at least tidy up the kitchen and dining room. I still had the best part of an hour, so could probably make the place reasonably respectable, and while I did so I knew I'd run through the same loop of self-interrogation. Which was pointless. I always felt a bit like this, didn't I? At this point in the process, with the full extent of a child's difficulties and attendant behaviour problems laid bare, invariably came a rush of regretful hindsight. They always say you never know someone till you live with them, don't they? And though I think it's an expression which is normally applied to marriage, the same very much applied to foster children. Perhaps more so, because it kind of went with the territory of getting to know them. They learned to build such high walls around themselves – that was so often their way of coping – and it was only the breaking down of them that brought the grim reality into view.

But I also knew, as far as Mike and I were concerned anyway, that Tyler wasn't going anywhere. I had known it that Saturday, because it would take much more than what he'd done to make me quit. Had had it confirmed an hour ago when I saw him sneak a peek into his lunchbox and do a little fist-pump on seeing the chocolate brownie I'd put in there – the same brownies he'd made such a show of not being 'bothered' about when I'd given him one fresh from the oven the day before. Little things, I thought, as I switched off the engine. Little increments.

John's car pulled up outside at precisely nine thirty, disgorging both him and a rangy-looking guy in T-shirt and jeans. This would be Will Fisher – Tyler's new social worker. He looked young – perhaps late twenties or early thirties, I guessed – with shoulder-length hair that my mum would have said needed someone to drag a comb through it. It was dark blond and wavy and looked faintly messianic and I decided he'd have looked equally at home with a

Casey Watson

guitar slung over his shoulder, fronting an indie band and crooning love songs to screaming teenage fans. I grinned to myself as I watched the pair shut the car doors. They were laughing at some shared joke over the roof as they did so, and knew I'd been right in thinking I hadn't previously met Will – I very much doubted that I would have forgotten him.

I was also glad he was young and male, because I felt there was a chance that Tyler would respond well to him. And that mattered a lot, as one of the first things John had promised was that Will would be taking Tyler out on a regular basis, both to get to know him (and hopefully foster another crucial positive adult relationship which would continue beyond his spell with us) and to give us what I already knew would be a much-needed break. And my hunch was that Tyler responded well to males. No, he'd not got off to the best start with my poor son, admittedly, but Kieron had since been back again – he and his girlfriend Lauren had stopped by for tea on the Tuesday, and I had felt a positive change in the dynamic. Was I being whimsical in sensing that Tyler wasn't just looking up *at* him; that he was wondering if he should look up *to* him too?

I mentally crossed my fingers that he might look up to Will as well. Not that you could second-guess that sort of thing about social workers really. They came in as many different varieties as did foster families, after all. There was no 'one size fits all' when it came to these kinds of careers. People went into them from all sorts of backgrounds, and with all sorts of motivations, and over the years I'd come across all sorts of different people, who brought all kinds of different things to the task at hand. One thing we all shared, however, was a common goal: to make the best of what, more often than not, was a pretty grim situation for whichever child was in our hands.

I went to the front door and opened it just as John was lifting his hand to press the bell, and as soon as I saw Will close up I decided I liked him. A snap judgement, yes, but I'd have been surprised if I'd have to revise it. And based on nothing more substantial than the slogan on his T-shirt – 'Imagine Whirled Peas!' – and the strength and immediacy of his handshake.

'So,' John said, after the usual introductions, 'Casey, how *are* you?' The emphasis was, I noted, very much on the 'are'. As it would be – he'd called for an update at the beginning of the week, and had certainly got one. 'And how's your dad doing?' he added, as I ushered them both in.

'Better than anyone expected, actually,' I told him as we went into the kitchen. As it was going to be just the three of us, there was more than enough space around the table, and the kitchen was the one room I always managed to keep on top of. 'Which is just as well, really,' I added, gesturing that they both sit down. 'Given that in just a fortnight we've had a broken door pane, a broken clock and the makings of the third world war.'

'Clock? Should I ask about the clock,' he ventured, 'or is this – ahem – a bad time?'

'I don't know,' I said, nudging him playfully. 'What *is* the time anyway? I have no means of telling any more, do I?'

'Er, I'll take that as a no, then,' John said, groaning, as I made coffee and Will began extracting paperwork from a big battered messenger bag. 'So will Mike be joining us?'

I shook my head. 'He would have done,' I said, 'but work's a bit manic at the moment. And given that the baptism of fire's already happened, there didn't seem much point in him taking time off.' I smiled at them both. 'And it's not as if he needs preparing for the worst, after all, is it? No, I'll update him on everything tonight.'

In fact, the broken clock was just a casualty of the third world war. Just on the wrong wall at the wrong time – i.e. in the vicinity of a door that Tyler had decided needed slamming – and, being a veteran anyway, had had its period of active service abruptly curtailed.

As opposed to Mike and I, who had by now discussed Tyler at length, and had decided we weren't quite ready to be put out to grass. No, by now we were back in the groove of having a pint-sized person dominating our lives, and finding out some facts would be grist to the mill.

Which I hoped we were about to get. Facts we could work with. 'So,' Will said, once we were seated and in possession of mugs of coffee, 'where shall I start?'

'At the beginning would be good,' I quipped, nudging the plate of biscuits in his direction. 'Because right now I feel we know almost nothing.'

Will made straight for a custard cream and popped the whole thing in his mouth, washing it down with a swig of coffee while he used his other hand to open the laptop that had emerged from his bag and now sprung into life.

'Well, he has told me bits and bats,' I clarified, as I marvelled at how relaxed and laid back this new social worker appeared to be. 'I know his real mum was called Fiona, and that all he's got to remind him of his early life now is a baby photo. And though he's not said as such, I get the impression that he does remember some of the harsher parts of his early years, I'm afraid. I mean, you do tend to hope that when things happen to them as mere tots they might forget about it as they grow older ...'

'You do,' John said as I drifted off with my sugar-coated thoughts. 'Unfortunately, when their life continues to be harsh – as in this case – however, the nasty things never get put to rest, do they? It's never too late though, is it? To give them a whole new set of memories and experiences. That's what we're hoping for with Tyler.'

'Assuming he can be kept out of trouble in the interim,' Will concluded, giving us both a wry smile. 'Which, from what I've read and heard, sounds like it'll be no mean feat, frankly.'

Which kind of burst the bubble. What exactly was *in* his files? 'Well, if anyone can keep him on the straight and narrow the Watsons can,' John told him loyally. 'So he's in a safe pair of hands, at least. *Finally*.'

I looked at John and smiled, acknowledging the compliment, but we both knew there was no such animal as a 'safe pair of hands' in our line of work. The only way to achieve that would be to put children like Tyler in secure units and lock the door behind them. And as we weren't in the business of incarceration that wasn't an option.

Not that I would ever want it to be, in any case. No, we were much more in the business of cause and effect and finding workable strategies to make progress, which meant I was much more interested in hearing about how a lad like Tyler came to be a lad like Tyler in the first place. Once we knew that, I knew we had a substantially better chance of helping him. There was so much locked inside him that needed to come out.

'Safe as we can make them,' I corrected. 'Though not fail-safe, by any means. So,' I added, turning to Will, 'how *did* Tyler's story begin, then?'

'Grimly,' came the unequivocal reply.

I knew all about grim, of course. We'd heard plenty of grim stories in our time, and I didn't expect this one to be any different. Kids from all sorts of backgrounds came into care, obviously – the abandoned, the tragically orphaned, the temporarily without a loving family able to take care of them – but there were constants; the stories that came up again and again and again – the stories and the words that made everyone sigh, not least because of their depressing ubiquity. Violence. Sexual abuse. Paedophilia. Drug addiction. Heroin.

And this was Tyler's word, apparently. Heroin. Heroin had been the loaded gun, circumstances the trigger. As Will explained, Tyler (who had been born some 30 miles away, and whose notes had followed him to us) had been born to a heroin-addicted mother. She had been around 21 when she'd had him, and because she had already been known to social services (she'd been in trouble with the police for possession since her mid-teens apparently), she'd been put on a methadone treatment programme during the pregnancy, in an effort both to wean her off the drug and its evils and to give her unborn baby the best chance.

Giving opiate-addicted mothers methadone was (and is) obviously a good thing, in that it was both an opportunity to take care of them and a step on the road to getting them off heroin permanently, but it still meant that their babies were born addicts as well. This was the case with Tyler, who was born with a condition called neonatal abstinence syndrome (or NAS), which meant that his first days were spent in hospital, while they slowly and carefully weaned him from the drug.

There were apparently no lasting side-effects to NAS – not physically. But how about emotionally? How did starting life with a recovering addict affect a baby? It was a sad but all too familiar story. There probably wasn't a foster family around who hadn't at some point come across the horrendous consequences of addiction to hard drugs, either directly or indirectly; the ripples of addiction always spread very wide.

'Though both mother and baby were apparently doing okay,' Will added, 'for a while there, it seems, at any rate. Mum – Fiona, as you say – wanted to turn her life around, get clean, do her best for the baby, and it seems that, with support, she did make a go of it at first.'

She must have done, I knew, because in that sort of situation the newborn child would almost always be taken straight into care. A new baby was upheaval enough for a mother who was well and supported, let alone one so young, so alone and so chronic a drug user. That she managed to cope for *any* length of time was remarkable in itself – a testament to both her and the professionals looking after her. I knew that from personal experience with my last foster child, Emma.

Thinking of Emma was what prompted me to ask my next question. 'So was Tyler's father around at this time?' I asked. 'Was he involved in all this?'

Will shook his head. 'No. Dad – Gareth – was most definitely out of the picture. At this point, no one even knew who he was, apparently. They'd split up early on – he maintained that he didn't even know about the pregnancy – and she apparently wanted nothing from him, in any case. No, such records as I've dug out seem to suggest she was managing adequately on her own at first.'

'What about other family?'

'None have been recorded. I've looked back through all the notes and it seems she was on her own. Living in a council property. Either no family, or estranged from them. No siblings or half-siblings, as far as anyone was aware.'

'So what went wrong? Was there some specific trigger?'

'Not that I can see,' Will said. 'The social worker's notes mention some concerns here and there, but on the whole she *was* doing okay. They seem to have concluded that it must have been a combination of aggravating factors. She got re-housed when the block she was living in was up for demolition, which could have been key, obviously – you know how it goes. Then a new man apparently came into her life … started her on the heroin again …'

'And surprise, surprise – it all went back downhill from there?' John asked.

It was phrased as a question, but we all knew it wasn't. She'd have been on benefits at that point, not to mention having her own flat. Which would have made her vulnerable. She'd have been a prime target for all sorts of parasites and predators.

'So Tyler was taken into care at that point?' I asked.

Will shook his head. 'No. Would that he had been, eh? No, it's worse than that. She was always just a hop and a skip away from that, of course – the previous social worker's made several notes about having concerns – but events seem to have overtaken that. She took a fatal overdose – at home, and probably unintentionally, the social worker thinks; possibly purer stuff than she was used to. And the first anyone knew of it was two days later, when she didn't turn up for a rehab appointment with her counsellor.'

'Oh, my God,' I said, shaking my own head now. 'That's so sad.'

'And it's lucky she had the appointment scheduled when she did,' he added, 'or it could have been even longer before they were found, couldn't it? As it was, the counsellor had the nous to go round there, thank goodness, and hearing crying from upstairs called the police.'

'Who then found Tyler …' I said.

Will nodded. 'And that's incredible as well, don't you think? Given his age. I mean, two whole days. It's incredible he didn't come to any harm in that time, isn't it? When you think about the environment he was in.'

Incredible, but at the same time the word 'harm' struck a chord. Yes, he'd survived that ordeal, but, God, he had come to *so* much harm since. 'So he was unhurt?' I asked. 'I mean, physically?'

Will nodded a second time. 'Emaciated, starving and traumatised, obviously – it's all in here; you can read it for yourself later – but otherwise, yes. And he was obviously put with emergency carers while they decided what best to do with him, and that's where the father comes in. With the help of some clues in a phone book and some donkey work, they managed to track him down – which was impressive in itself, because he'd by now moved to this area – and he agreed (I believe reluctantly) that he and his partner would take Tyler on rather than him being placed with a foster family.'

'Which is interesting in itself, isn't it?' John said. 'I mean, given that he said he didn't even know about the existence of a baby. Does it say anything in there about him wanting the paternity proven?'

'There was certainly a test done,' Will said, 'though I think we instigated it, for the usual reasons. They wouldn't have just handed Tyler over, even if they'd welcomed him with open arms. And they kept tabs on the family for the usual span of time. And from what I've read in here,' he said, patting the file, 'it seems he stepped up to the plate readily enough. That he was the father wasn't apparently in doubt anyway, looking at the other child. Apparently they were the spit of each other.' He sat back in his chair, then leaned in again and grabbed another biscuit. 'So that was that, in theory. Taken off the "at risk" register, and settled back with blood relatives. The only trouble is that it's obviously not worked out all *that* brilliantly, has it?'

Hmm, I thought. *You can say that again.*

Chapter 6

Meeting Will, and hearing first hand about Tyler's early childhood, was just the kick up the backside I think we needed. Yes, we'd already committed to him and, heaven knew, we'd had enough training, hadn't we? Enough training to have 'It's the behaviour that's bad, not the child' mentally tattooed on our foreheads. But the image of that traumatised three-year-old, all alone with the body of his dead mother, was one that stuck firmly to the forefront of my brain.

'And you know what always strikes me?' I told Riley one afternoon the following week. 'It's that he doesn't even seem to realise that he's been handed such a bad hand.'

Tyler being out for his first trip with Will – they were off to the local bowling alley – we were round at Mum and Dad's, enjoying a bit of family time with the baby, which only served to remind me how random a child's birth circumstances were. Some babies were born into loving, stable homes. And some weren't. Some had everything stacked against them from the outset.

'Life's been so tough for him,' I went on. 'I don't think he really appreciates just *how* tough. Or that it's the adults in his life that are responsible for how he now feels. He just doesn't seem to have processed that. Turns everything on himself. Seems to feel it's perfectly appropriate for people not to like him. It's like he just accepts that he's angry and wants everybody else to as well.' I sighed. 'I just wish I could find a way to get him to talk to me about it. But it really is like trying to get blood out of a stone. I only have to look at him in a certain way and I can see him squirming. I swear he has some sixth sense that tells him when I'm about to corner him and try and talk to him. Perhaps he's like a dog – he can smell a heart-to-heart on the horizon like they can smell fear.'

Riley clapped her hands together. 'Love it, Mum!' she laughed. But she then moved on to her serious face, clearly thinking about the problem. At 27, she was the polar opposite of Kieron, though. Where my son would see everything on the surface and immediately have a practical solution or suggestion, Riley was a deep, thoughtful thinker. Like me, she always tried to look beyond what you could see. She was good at it, too, and until taking a bit of a break after having had Marley Mae she and her partner David had been fostering as well – providing respite care for the same agency that we worked for.

Passing the baby across to my mum for a cuddle, she smiled at me. 'Well, you know what to do about that, Mum, don't you?'

I raised my eyebrows as she continued to fuss over my youngest grandchild. 'I do?'

'Course you do,' she said. 'Do what you used to do with me and Kieron. Trap him in the car. Take him off for a drive somewhere and drone on at him while he can't escape.'

'God, you make it sound like a form of torture,' I said, shaking my head at my amused mother.

Riley laughed. 'It was! Felt like that sometimes, at any rate. I swear, sometimes me and Kieron used to sweat at the jangle of your car keys.'

'Oh you do exaggerate, Riley,' I admonished. She was right, though. I did remember doing just that. And she was spot on; sometimes it probably did feel like a kind of torture – especially if the subject matter was at all sensitive: affairs of the heart, drugs and rock 'n' roll, sex …

And it worked. Even if you didn't always see the evidence at the time, there was a lot to be said for putting kids in a position where they didn't have to make eye contact with you. It made it easier for them to talk. And it made it harder for them not to listen.

I still did it, too, with foster kids – albeit almost unconsciously these days. And Riley was right. I'd not yet thought about it, but it was exactly what I should do with Tyler. Because if I was to help him, I really needed to understand better where all that rage and hurt and self-loathing had come from.

And it didn't take a brain surgeon to reach the conclusion that the relationship with his stepmother was probably key. Though I had nothing to go on bar the rather vague detail on Tyler's file that 'relations had broken down' with his father's partner, I was itching to get an inkling of what form this breakdown had taken. More to the point, when had it started? Had something specific prompted it? Something Tyler had done? I was particularly intrigued by what sort of conversations must have happened early on, between the father who'd been told he had a son who he'd never known existed, and the partner with which he'd had another son in the meantime, and who might have had her own ideas about the situation in which – through no fault of her own – she now found herself.

I tried to relate it to me. How would *I* have felt if Mike had come home from work one evening and announced that he had another child I hadn't known about? What would my reaction have been if he then told me I would have to welcome it into our family and raise it?

I didn't know. That was the honest answer. I didn't have a clue how I'd have reacted. First, I'd have to accept that he really didn't know anything about it, and then … well, and then I'd have to do a great deal of soul-searching, wouldn't I? About my capacity to not only accept this sudden cuckoo-in-the-nest into my home but to commit to loving it and cherishing it to the best of my ability; to bringing it up as if it were my own.

Of course, I wanted to think that, yes, I *would* be able to do that. After all, falling in love with the kids we fostered was both my blessing *and* my curse. It was emotionally draining every time, quite apart from anything else. So, yes, on balance, had it been Mike, and had the circumstances been the same ones, I wanted to think that I would embrace the child – because it would have been *his* child, and a half-sibling to his other children too, which would have meant I would have no hesitation. It would be the right thing to do.

But this wasn't me, was it? And life was rarely that simple and rosy. With her own child just a toddler, was this Alicia coping okay anyway? Could it be that, actually, she *was* managing, but that she really didn't want to take on any more? Was she pressured by Tyler's father to take him in? Pressured by social services? Pressured by knowing that if she didn't agree to have him, she would feel like a bad person for the rest of her life? Not the best reason to take on another woman's child.

What with dashing around to help my mum, and life being so busy generally, it was to be another week before the ideal opportunity presented itself. It was almost the end of term now – the long summer holidays looming provocatively, close on the horizon – and as I watched Tyler mooching out of school one afternoon, deep in conversation with another lad, I was idly wondering how it must feel to *be* him. He'd been with us a few weeks now, and we were managing – just – to keep a lid on his behaviour, but, as for getting close to him, progress was proving slow. There had been so many times when I automatically reached out to connect with him physically, but he'd always shrink back, stiffen slightly, send out unambiguous signals. Had this kid ever been hugged in his young life? Perhaps yes, by his real mother, but since then? I decided probably not.

And Will had reported much the same. Not that he was offering to cuddle him, but though Tyler had pronounced him 'cool' and better than the previous 'bossy old bag', Will himself still felt that sense of distance, of careful guardedness in Tyler; that he was only chipping, bit by tiny bit, away. Time, we'd both agreed – that would be the key. Time and patience. He'd surely let us in eventually.

I watched him now and wondered, though. What went on behind those big brown eyes? Under that mop of inky hair? I wondered something else, too. I wondered what it must feel like to be his stepmother. That, I felt, was key to understanding how we'd got to where we'd got – to her taking what by any yardstick was extremely drastic action – taking her own son's half-brother to court. I would probably never know that, I realised. It wasn't my business to know that, anyway. But it seemed that I was about to get an inkling.

'So,' I said to Tyler, as he threw his backpack into the back seat of the car and tumbled in behind it, 'how was school today? Okay?'

'All right,' came the expected grunt of a response.

'Good,' I said. 'At least that's an improvement on "rubbish".' Which was what the grunt of a response had been the previous day. 'Anyway,' I added, suddenly hatching a plan. 'I have good news. You're coming with me to the supermarket, okay? The big out-of-town one. And we're going to go straight there. And before you pull a face' – I added, peering into the rear-view mirror – 'I've had a busy day with the grandkids and I haven't had time to go yet, so, in fact, it's your lucky day –'

'Lucky?' Tyler huffed. 'Going to buy food and crap?'

'Language,' I chided, 'and yes, going to buy food and stuff, which will give you the opportunity to earn some "being helpful" points for your daily sheet, and, if you are really helpful, I might even treat you to a DVD from the bargain stand by the till.'

I noticed Tyler had already retrieved his mobile phone from his bag and was now busy tapping away on some game or other. 'And you'll need those points if you're hoping to top that flipping phone up at the weekend, won't you?'

I wasn't being completely honest about the 'falling behind' aspect of my day. Though it was true that I had been longer at Mum's than I planned, and that I needed to keep Saturday free to help her with all her chores, it had just hit me that a trip to the supermarket would be the ideal situation for a chat. In the car ... pushing the trolley round ... back in the car again ... And even if he didn't open up that much – and he mightn't – it would be good for him to help me out domestically anyway. And perhaps taking him shopping and letting him have some input – choosing his preferred cereal and squash and maybe a couple of choices for dinner the following week – would all help with the business of him feeling less threatened, and realising that our only wish was to take care of him until his life settled back down.

And, for a while at least, it seemed it was going to.

'You know mash?' he said, growing more chatty with every aisle we went down.

'I do know mash,' I said. 'I've probably made more saucepans of mash than you've had hot dinners.'

'Well, d'you ever get salad cream and, like, make a hole in the middle and then get tuna fish and put both in the middle and make a volcano?'

I pulled a face. 'Erm, not lately, it must be said. Why – is it nice?'

'It's epic,' he said. 'You should try it. It's me an' Grant's most favourite tea in the universe. When we're on our own, like, and we've only got what's in the cupboards, that's what we always make.'

I made a mental note of the word 'alone'. At their ages? 'You mean, you peel your own potatoes and everything?' I said. 'I am seriously impressed. Remind me to pop that on your chart.'

But he was shaking his head. 'Nah, not normally – not when it's just us. We use the Smash stuff. You know – the one you just put water on and stir it.'

'Ah,' I said. 'I know it well. "For mash, get Smaaaaaaash …"'

He looked at me as if I'd completely lost my marbles.

'It's an old TV ad,' I explained. 'With aliens and … no. Perhaps not. Never mind. But we will get some tuna fish and some extra salad cream, as well, and … Tyler?' I finished, realising I'd suddenly lost his attention. I turned to follow his gaze beyond me. 'Tyler – *what*?'

At a pinch, in dim light, you could put two and two together. With us both having black hair and brown eyes, it wouldn't have been beyond the bounds of possibility to think we were mother and son. Or, okay, if you were feeling less charitable, grandmother and son. It had been Kieron who'd pointed it out and it had tickled me. All those kids we'd fostered – both short and long term – and this was the first time we'd had a child in who looked so much like me. But when I turned around to see what it was that had so transfixed Tyler, it was to find myself looking at a lad who *really* looked like Tyler – so much so that there wasn't a shred of indecision in my mind. In a dim light they could almost be twins. This had to be the very little brother who we'd just been discussing.

It was. 'Yo, Grant!' Tyler called, slipping out from behind the trolley he'd been pushing for me, and jogging the ten feet or so that separated them in the washing powder aisle. It was a perfectly natural and perfectly obvious reaction to seeing him, and for half a second I smiled and thought – 'Ahh, how nice is that?' Specially when the two boys briefly hugged.

It didn't even strike me as any sort of incredible coincidence; I already knew the family didn't live a long way away from us, and though that was unusual – you didn't usually foster kids who lived very close to you – it was always going to be odds on they might shop here from time to time.

But within another half second I realised that the other boy wasn't on his own. A few yards behind him there was a woman, not pushing a trolley but carrying a basket, and who was now standing stock still, bar the hand that she'd lifted to her face, and with which she was looping a hank of blonde hair behind her ear.

Then she spoke. 'Grant! Come back here!' I heard her call to him. The tension in her voice thrummed towards me on the air.

'Grant!' she said again, at which point he turned back towards her, uncertain. And it was then that I knew, beyond any shred of doubt, that we were going to have a scene. That there would be a kicking off.

I took in the details, realising that she was not as I'd imagined her. She was young – probably late twenties, no more than that – very tall and lean, with the sort of pinched look that set bells ringing in my brain straight away, but which thought I pushed away. Who was I to make assumptions? I didn't know anything about her, did I?

'Mu-*um*,' Grant was saying, as he and Tyler drew level, and I watched older and younger brother greet each other with evident pleasure. I pushed the trolley towards them and plastered on a breezy smile. I wasn't exactly going to say 'Well, fancy meeting you here!' but I felt that something along those lines would probably do. Show the boys that we could play nicely. At least that's what I'd intended. But something told me she didn't want to speak to me. She certainly didn't seem to want to meet my eye.

'Grant, will you do as you're *fucking* told!' she snapped, causing the heads of the other couple of people cruising the aisles to duly snap up in surprise. 'And come right back here this minute!'

At which point I might have said something conciliatory – there was really no need for that sort of response, surely? But Tyler beat me to it.

'He can talk to me if he fucking wants to,' he roared at her, 'so leave us alone, you bitch!'

'Tyler!' I started, reaching to grab a hold of him. It was almost automatic. And he was ready for it, and wrestled his arm free.

'Leave me alone!' he screeched back at me. 'He's my fucking little brother! I can talk to him if I want to! *She* can't fucking stop me!'

Except, obviously, she could. The aisle cleared, then, one pensioner even breaking into a trot. 'Tyler,' I said again, firmly but not aggressively. 'Don't make this worse than it already is, okay? Come on, come away ...'

But he completely ignored me. For all the things that he was and might be – he was still something of an unknown quantity – he was never slow in coming forward, and he was brave. He marched up to her and, though she was taller than him by a good seven or eight inches, jabbed an angry finger towards her chest.

'They'll get you!' he told her, while his younger brother kept casting anxious glances at me. 'They'll get you! They *fucking* will, you witch!'

His little brother was by now tugging on the sleeve of his school sweatshirt. 'Ty,' he was saying, 'stop it! Please, Ty – just leave it!'

'Tyler,' I said, grabbing his wrist again, 'come on. Come *away*.' I looked at his stepmother, who finally met my eyes and rolled her own. *You see?* they seemed to be saying to me. *You see what I have to deal with?* And before she could get a word out he played right into it too, swinging a leg back, then hammering his foot into her shin. Now she did speak.

'For Christ's sake!' she said, mostly to me, finally. 'He's a fucking *animal*!'

'I'm so sorry,' I said, because I didn't really know what else *to* say. 'Come on, Tyler. Come on, let's get you home. Come on, you have to *stop* this.'

'Too bloody right!' his stepmother said, bending down to rub her shin. 'Jesus Christ, I can't even go into the supermarket without being fucking *assaulted* … Grant, will you get right here, *now*!'

He scuttled to her side and, having at last got a firm grip on Tyler, I left the trolley parked by the fabric conditioners and dragged him away.

The duty manager intercepted us just as we'd cleared the fruit and veg. 'Is everything all right?' he wanted to know, looking anxiously from me to Tyler and back again.

'Everything's fine,' I reassured him brightly. 'Isn't it, love?' I added. I didn't loosen my grip on Tyler, not even a little. Then, before the man could ask anything further I sidestepped him and left them to it. We'd perhaps come back and do the shopping another day.

And as I walked Tyler to the car – he was crying now, but I pretended I didn't know that – I remembered that thing car insurance companies always say you should do in the event of an accident. That, even if you know the prang is your fault, you should never say sorry, because that's the same as admitting liability. That you should never do that, because that's for *them* to decide.

This was like that, I decided. Just the same sort of thing. And though I couldn't quite put my finger on why it mattered to me so greatly, I really wished that I hadn't said that sorry.

Chapter 7

It was a 15-minute drive from the supermarket to home, but as I ushered Tyler back up the front path I realised that it wasn't only him who was still feeling agitated – my own heart was still pumping with adrenalin. No, it hadn't actually flared up into a full-blown physical tussle, thank goodness, but it had been an ugly, disturbing scene and, more than that, a telling one. It had told me a great deal about the state of affairs in Tyler's home – none of which filled me with much hope.

And it seemed events were moving on apace now, as well. As I put my key in the door I could hear the house phone ringing.

'Go on, love,' I said to Tyler. 'Get upstairs and change out of your uniform while I get that. Then come straight back down. You and I need to have a chat, okay?'

Tyler, no doubt glad to be off the leash, ran off up the stairs as instructed, while I made a grab for the phone.

It was John Fulshaw. 'Ah, you're there,' he said. 'I was just about to hang up.'

'Sorry,' I gasped into the receiver, 'long story. How are you?'

'I have mixed news to give you, I'm afraid,' John said, without preamble. 'The good news is that Will Fisher has agreed to do an extra half day a week with Tyler during the school holidays – assuming that suits you, of course – take him off on some outings – swimming, go-karting; that sort of thing. Thought it might give you a bit of extra breathing space.'

'That *is* good news,' I said. And for me as well as Tyler. I wasn't Methuselah, but neither was I a spring chicken these days, and what with the holidays approaching, and with trying to support Riley through those intense early months with my gorgeous but demanding grand-daughter, those few hours a week to catch my breath would be welcome indeed. 'But what's the flip side? Go on. I'm braced.'

'It's not *that* bad,' John reassured me. 'Just a little unexpected. I've just taken another call from Will – just as I was going to ring you with the first news, funnily enough – to say they have Tyler's court date, and it's rather short notice. Which is no problem for them – they already have their case organised, and it's obviously a strong one – but it doesn't leave a lot of time for you and Mike to put something together – you know, as in what we talked about? Just a few illustrative snippets to show how he's doing; how he's remorseful, keen to make amends and so on.'

'Of course,' I said. 'But exactly how short are we talking about here?'

'It's next Wednesday. 11.00 a.m.,' he said. 'You know where the courts are, don't you?'

Jeepers, I thought. That *was* pretty short notice. 'Next Wednesday! That's less than a week away! Yes, I know where the courts are,' I added, 'but, oh dear, I have to tell you that we've had something of an incident this afternoon – which I think might just upset the apple-cart a bit.'

I explained to John about what had happened following our encounter in the supermarket, and how it had given me more of an idea of what we were up against. 'And the frustrating thing is that this could happen again, couldn't it? With the family living so close by, we could end up bumping into them all the time.'

Which, given what had happened, was now becoming a worry, for obvious reasons. The way Tyler's stepmother had been with him spoke volumes. It was the clearest indication yet that she really wanted nothing more to do with him – not to mention how she obviously felt about letting him near his little brother, which was the thing that had saddened me most of all.

And made me determined to try and get something more out of him – particularly about the night in question – so we'd at least have a fuller picture of what we were up against, come the hearing. 'Leave it with me,' I told John. 'Don't worry – we'll get something together. I'll also run through the court procedure with Tyler so that he's prepared for what'll happen. Maybe after what's happened this afternoon he'll feel a little more like talking anyway. I really hope so. That poor lad needs to fight his corner.'

'Er, not literally, Casey,' John corrected. 'That's how we got to this, remember!'

John was right. But Tyler needed someone to fight his corner for him, and, in that respect, I knew I was number one candidate. I also had an hour before Mike was due home so it was time to start tea, and I intended to put it to good use.

'Come on, love,' I called up the stairs to Tyler, once I'd said goodbye to John. 'I need to talk to you. Don't worry,' I added, when he didn't appear, 'you're not in trouble.'

There was still no response, and I'd already mounted the first couple of stairs when Tyler appeared at the top of them. It was obvious he'd been crying, and trying to wipe away the evidence. My heart went out to him. 'I'm not?' he said. 'You *promise* I'm not?'

'Absolutely not,' I reassured him, as I beckoned him back down. I felt a rush of positivity. This was exactly what I'd been waiting for. Not that I wanted him upset and crying, of course, but I did want a way in. A tiny chink in the armour. A little glimpse into the heart of the hurt kid that I knew lay behind the cloak of attitude and anger. 'I promise, sweetie,' I said again as he started to walk slowly down the stairs. 'No, you shouldn't have lashed out physically – but you already know that, don't you? But, apart from that, you have nothing to reproach yourself for. It's not *your* fault that we bumped into them, is it? And, as far as I can see, it's not your fault that you weren't allowed to speak to your brother, either.'

Which I knew, even as I said it, wasn't perhaps the most appropriate thing for me to be saying to him. My normal world was one in which adults, in the main, knew best, hung together and were of largely similar opinions – the world where if a child came home and said that their teacher had told them off, it was natural to assume it must have been for a good reason. And, in truth, I didn't know. Perhaps there was a very good reason why Tyler wasn't allowed to speak to his little brother – perhaps he had 'previous' with him, as well. But my instinct screamed otherwise. If there was a good reason for Tyler to be denied contact with his sibling, then I felt 100 per cent sure it would already be in the notes somewhere – as extra ammunition, fired by his stepmother, in the cause of taking him to court. But there was nothing. Which spoke volumes to me.

So I didn't care, I decided – not on this occasion, anyway. This particular kid had already been through enough. 'Come on,' I said, daring for the first time to ruffle his hair as he walked past, 'let's have a sit down, shall we? And have a proper chat.'

Tyler scrubbed at his eyes roughly as he took a seat at the dining table. I'd hoped he might head for the living room and get comfortable on the sofa, so that I could join him, but perhaps he wasn't ready for that level of physical closeness yet. And much as I wanted to give him a cuddle, his brittle little body told me I needed to bide my time for a bit. At least he was here with me, and his tears were progress in themselves; tears of hurt he was finally letting me see.

I sat down opposite him and folded my arms on the table. 'That phone call I just took was from my link worker, Tyler. You remember John, who brought you here?'

Tyler nodded and sniffed, and as he did so I noticed something else. He'd changed into his favourite hoodie, but the hood, for once, was down.

'Well,' I continued, deciding to leave Will out of things for the moment, 'he was calling to tell me that they now have a date for your court appearance.'

I watched as a look of panic crossed his features. 'It's next Wednesday,' I added quickly, 'but, Tyler, that's a *good* thing. It's better that it's so soon. It means it'll be over and done with – so you won't have it hanging over you, making you worry.'

'But that's less than a week away!' he cried, parroting what I'd just said to John. 'They'll send me down, won't they? I know they will.'

I would have smiled at his choice of term if I had felt at all like smiling. As it was, I was more concerned with reassuring him. 'Tyler, they won't be "sending you down". They won't be sending you anywhere,' I added, crossing my fingers that I was right. But how could I not be? He was 11. There couldn't be a magistrate in the land that would countenance such a thing, surely? And if we were unlucky enough to find one who felt differently, I'd take it upon myself to appeal in the strongest terms. Chain myself to the court railings, if need be, I decided. Or the bike rack, more likely. But it would be unnecessary. He'd already been sent 'down' after all – down into the care system. Down to our house.

Which, to my mind, was the first positive in the whole sorry business. 'How do you know?' he argued. 'One of my mates threatened this old lady with a knife once, and he got sent away for *ever*.'

'Don't be daft, love. They won't send you away,' I said, 'I promise you. Sweetie, what you did was done in the heat of the moment. You were angry about so many things, weren't you?' He nodded slightly. 'Whereas your friend – well, I'm just guessing, but I bet that was completely different. If he threatened some poor old lady with a knife, then he probably deserved to get sent away, didn't he? But I can assure you it won't have been for ever.'

Tyler looked like he was about to burst into tears again – which was no surprise, really, if he'd been harbouring a conviction that his fate was to be flung into jail. I needed to steer the conversation to a safer place for him. 'Look, sweetie,' I went on, 'John also called to tell me that the social workers are going to try and help you. They will have written letters that they'll read out in court to tell people about you – about what happened that night, and about other bad things that happened to you – the things that happened when you were little. Do you understand that?'

'D'you mean about my mum dying?'

'Yes, about your mum,' I said, nodding. 'And about *how* she died, too. And also about anything else they might know about anything that could have hurt you. That's what they'll be there for. You know, if you've told them stuff already, or to the police – you probably spoke to the police about it, didn't you? Well, they'll have it all written down and they'll tell everyone about it, to try to help the judge understand why you might have acted as you did.'

It was clearly a lot for him to take in, the idea that anyone might want to help him. But once he had, another thought had obviously struck him. 'But the judge prob'ly won't believe them,' he said, with feeling. '*She lies*, Casey! All the time! She tells all sorts of lies, and everyone *always* believes her. She'll tell them how bad I am and how good *she* is and that'll be that,' he finished. 'Ten years for me!'

I did suppress a smile at that, because he sounded just like the Artful Dodger. And with those big soulful eyes, he even looked a bit like him, too. But it really wasn't funny to see just how convinced he was that that would happen. 'Not at all!' I said firmly. 'Courts are not stupid, Tyler. They have to listen to *both* sides of every story. That's their job. Doesn't matter if it's a kid or an adult – they listen to everyone equally. And only then do they make up their mind who they believe the most.'

'An' they'll believe her!' he persisted.

'Not if they haven't got very good reason to,' I countered. 'And not if they have very good reason to believe *you*. Which is where social services come in, and where Mike and I come in, too. Tyler, we *know* all about the bad things that happened to you when you were little, and we're here to help you – you know that, don't you? To help make things better for you in any way we can. And one of the things I have to do next Wednesday is read out my own letter to the court – just like the helping letters I just mentioned – telling them how you've been feeling since you came to us. So what we need to do now is see if there's anything else you'd like them to know about you. Anything at all. About that night with the knife, or about any trouble *before* that night happened … anything that's happened … anything that's been done to you … anything that made you upset, made you feel so angry, perhaps – even something you might now feel sorry about having said or done … or any other feelings you might have, about *any* of it. Anything that's niggling you – about your dad and step-mum, about your brother, about your real mum … about *anything*, okay? And I'll sit and listen, and I'll remember what you tell me, then I'll write my letter for the court and I'll show it to you, okay? And then, assuming you're happy with what I put, I can read it out on Wednesday, to help the courts understand you a bit more.'

He pondered this for a few moments, a little crease forming on his forehead. 'But why do they want to understand me?' he asked, in a small, thoughtful voice. 'How would that help?'

I risked reaching across and ruffling his hair again, and I was thrilled when he didn't flinch. 'Because, sweetie, *everything* happens for a reason. It might seem like you did what you did just because you couldn't control your temper, but you know – and *I* know – there's more to it than that, isn't there? And we want the judge to know that as well, don't we? So,' I finished, hoping that his fear of 'going down' would prove the catalyst for him opening up, 'do you want to give it a go? Do you want to tell me?'

* * *

By the time the morning of the court case came around the following Wednesday, I looked in the bathroom mirror and decided I looked as if I'd aged by half a decade. I had hardly slept, and had bags under my eyes the size of suitcases – the baggage, I decided wryly, that I had finally wrestled out of Tyler, and clearly stashed in a convenient, but gallingly visible, location.

I would shove a couple of teaspoons in the freezer, I decided, and, once they were nicely chilled, give myself five uninterrupted minutes with them on my face. Because today was a day when I would need to be on song and look on top of things, particularly given the circumstances of the court case. I needed to look sharp and in control – not like a woman who was worn down by the stress of trying to manage this apparently *un*manageable, knife-wielding young thug.

No. This was Tyler's day of reckoning and he was counting on us to fight his corner, just as I had promised him we'd do. To advocate for him and to make sure the rest of his youth wouldn't be tainted by the outcome of today. Yes, he had done wrong, and he knew it. No one should ever take a weapon to another person – especially not a knife, which could inflict such serious damage – but both Mike and I, and social services, had to make sure that the court understood the extreme circumstances that had driven him to do such a thing. Make them aware that it wasn't just a violent over-reaction to whatever had happened between him and his stepmother that morning. That it was so much more than that, as I'd always suspected and now truly believed. The culmination of a process that had been started in his infancy – the combination of the severe trauma of losing his mother the way he did, and a subsequently crappy upbringing – there was no other word for it.

It was still only 7.00 a.m. when I slipped quietly out of the shower and temporarily into a pair clean pyjamas. I would need to get dolled up in smart, court-appropriate clothing, but there was no rush, and, besides, I didn't want to wake anyone just yet, especially Mike – I'd already kept him awake until the early hours going over everything as it was. He deserved a bit more sleep – it was a rare Wednesday off work for him after all, and an even rarer lie-in – and as we weren't due in court until 11.00 a.m. there was plenty of time for him to enjoy another hour's kip.

No, I decided, I'd let both of them sleep, and while they did so I would go downstairs to cook up a special breakfast for us all. And I was almost at the fridge, with the intention of getting eggs, bacon and mushrooms out, when a slight movement at the edge of my vision made me almost jump out of my skin.

'Oh, my goodness!' I gasped, realising that it was Tyler who I was seeing. He was squatting down, with his back to the cupboard next to the fridge-freezer, partly obscured behind the kitchen table and chairs. 'What on earth are you doing up this early? And fully dressed too! And why are you hiding down there?'

'I wasn't hiding,' he responded, rising. 'I was just sitting an' thinking.' He looked thoroughly miserable, too. I pulled a chair out and made him sit on it, reflecting on how young and vulnerable he looked in the clothes I'd laid out ready the night before. School trousers, white shirt, school shoes – nicely polished – topped off with a smart V-necked jumper I'd found for him, court being no place for his beloved hoodies.

'Thinking what?' I asked him, reaching into the fridge for the breakfast things, trying to keep everything light.

'That I'm scared, Casey,' he said. 'I'm not never going home, am I? Not after you read them court people the stuff that I told you. I shouldn't have told you it. I wish I hadn't now. She'll hate me more than ever now, and make Dad hate me too.'

My heart went out to him, and I went straight to sit beside him. He was caught between a rock and a hard place, and there was nothing I could say or do that would change that. He needed to make his case, and he knew that. He needed the court to know the truth. But at the same time, in the telling, he had made himself vulnerable – handed her even more reason to push him out of their lives. And since I'd met her myself in the supermarket, I was sure that was her plan.

It was a stark place to be and I wished he didn't have to be there. In that instant I felt a flame of fury flare towards his father. Where had *he* been? Why hadn't he seen what must have been happening for so long? Why had he not protected his son? Here was this broken kid, who clearly loved his dad and his brother with all his heart. But between them and him was this obstacle who appeared to be determined that he wouldn't be part of their lives. And to compound the problem, this obstacle was loved and cherished by both the father and the brother, by all accounts, so Tyler really was the piggy in the middle.

And he was probably right. Today would only serve to reinforce that. Today would ensure that his stepmother would dislike him even more. Which affected me and how I handled things, clearly. I knew I would have to think very hard about what I said in that courtroom and how I said it.

'None of us know that, love,' I reassured him now, trying to put a positive spin on things. 'For all we know she might not even turn up to court. And even if she does, she might not get the chance to say anything at all. They might already have all the notes they need, mightn't they? And make a decision there and then. No point worrying about things we don't know, sweetie, is there? Now how about you jump up and help me cook us a big fry-up, eh? To keep us going. We'll surprise Mike. How about that?'

Helping me cook breakfast seemed to do the trick of taking his mind off things, even if only temporarily, and by half past ten – Tyler and Mike with full tummies and me with a full heart – the three of us were being ushered into a small room in the family court building.

Once in there, John explained to us that, because of Tyler's age, it was to be a special hearing in a room only a little larger than the one we were currently squashed into. Which was a relief. I had been in juvenile courts before – this one included – and they could be scary and intimidating places.

'As far as I know,' he explained, 'they also already have all the background they need.' He nodded towards Tyler at this point, and smiled at him. 'All the stuff about Mum and how you ended up at Dad's?' he qualified. Tyler nodded.

John looked back at Mike and me then. 'And they are also aware of some of the circumstances of the last few years.' He paused then, looking slightly uncomfortable. So I knew that whatever was coming next wouldn't necessarily be good news. And I wasn't wrong. 'One thing, though, Casey,' he added, 're what I've asked you to prepare, is that I've been told that the emphasis is going to be very much on the here and now – how Tyler feels about the actual incident with the knife. Whether he realises it was wrong and whether he's sorry about it – which I know you are, son,' he added, smiling again at Tyler. 'You know how it goes … busy schedule. Time tight and all that. So it looks like we won't have much of an opportunity to discuss the past. Just where he goes from here, I imagine.'

It was a cryptic thing to say, and my first thought was *what?* All those words Tyler had told me and that it had broken my heart to write – and then type – for him. Words that I had been holding tightly on to, both in my head and in my hands.

Words like '*Grant calls them "Mum and Dad", but I'm not allowed to. I have to use their proper names.*' Words like '*When Dad works away on the rigs she always hits me.*' Words like '*When Dad was at work, I had to go out robbing biscuits and stuff with Cameron when he did his paper round, cos she wouldn't let me have any breakfast.*' And the worst words of all: '*She grabbed me by the throat and said I was a fucking druggie's kid and nobody loved kids from druggies.*' I felt a lump rise in my throat thinking about some of the things Tyler had told me.

And now, just as he'd predicted, his words wouldn't even be heard.

But then another thought hit me, and it was altogether more positive. Could it be that the court had already kind of made their minds up? Could it be that, having heard what social services had to say, they already knew this was something of a waste of the court's time? That they could see beyond the crime of passion to the circumstances around it and, just maybe, have realised that this child was a product of those circumstances and that there were other ways to turn him around way better than 'sending him down'?

I hoped so. Oh, how I hoped so, particularly while I had to sit there and watch Tyler's stepmother (through tightly gritted teeth) dabbing her eyes and shaking her head as she told her tale of woe; talk in gentle tones of how she'd tried so incredibly hard with this 'unexpected' child of her husband's, but to no avail. He'd never loved her, she cried, no matter how much of a mother she tried to be. She *did* love him – she'd always tried to love him, just as if he were her own son – but as things were, she simply couldn't put her younger son or herself at risk of his violent outbursts any more. No, she concluded, for the foreseeable future anyway, sad to say it, he was much better off in care.

As she finished, I glanced at Tyler and saw the look of confusion on his face. He was just staring at her as if finding it impossible to reconcile what he was hearing with what he knew to be true. And that he had told me the truth I was in no doubt. 'Thank God we saw them in that supermarket,'

I hissed at Mike as she took her seat again. 'Because if we hadn't, she might have convinced me, as well.'

Mike squeezed my hand. 'I don't think so, love,' he said. 'She didn't convince me one bit. The thing is, has she convinced the magistrate? That's what matters.'

All I could do was hope not – not that it really mattered. Yes, there was an outside chance they'd opt for some sort of custodial order, but it was minuscule – no, what upset me more was the fact that Tyler had just had it spelt out to him so baldly that, as things stood, he was not welcome home. How must that make him feel? And was his dad not going to have any say in the matter? I guessed not; she was clearly speaking for the both of them. So far – and we'd not even been introduced to him, for God's sake – he'd been like a ghost – present, but not so you'd know it.

Will Fisher was up next, talking about how he was getting to know Tyler – of how well he always behaved with him, and how much empathy he displayed.

'And I'm not just relating my own experience,' he added, sounding reassuringly professional. 'As Tyler's social worker, I've also interviewed several others who have had dealings with him, including Tyler's previous social worker' – he outlined the maternity leave situation – 'and both his class teacher and the head of his new secondary school.' He then started to launch into some background information, only to be stopped in his tracks by a court official telling him they were aware of the family circumstances.

Was that a good thing or a bad thing? I didn't know, and I didn't think Will did either, but he pressed on, albeit looking a bit flustered, reporting that Tyler had shown a marked improvement in all areas, was settling down well in his new school and, despite earlier reports from his previous school, was indeed showing definite signs of remorse and a desire to please, plus a willingness to work hard on his temper.

Then, all of a sudden, it seemed to be my turn. I glanced down at the now slightly screwed-up notes in front of me and pondered what best to do. I knew what I had to do if I wanted to make Tyler's case properly, but I also knew that Tyler himself wasn't going to be too impressed at what I now realised he would see as throwing him to the lions as far as having any hope of making peace with his dad and brother was concerned. So I made a judgement. I would play the game and trust that enough had already been done to ensure nothing bad was going to happen. I cleared my throat and glanced nervously across the table at John, hoping he would make sense of my thinking.

'I'm Tyler's foster carer,' I explained, once I'd stepped up to what passed for a witness box, but was in fact just a long bench situated in front of the important people, and reserved – I imagined – for the witnesses such as myself, 'and during the short time he's been with us we've discussed this incident in detail. And, as a consequence, I can say with confidence that Tyler does indeed realise that what he did that night was wrong. He realises that to take a knife to anyone is against the law, and he is sorry. He knows that he will have to pay for it in some way, and he accepts that. He also realises …' I looked pointedly at Alicia here, before continuing, 'that no matter *what* circumstances led to that argument and fight, he still shouldn't have picked up a knife, no matter how angry he felt. I'd just like to ask that, if you do make an order today, it can be carried out within the home – *our* home, as things currently stand – and that Tyler is able to prove that he intends to change his life.'

'Thank you,' said the same court official that had cut Will short minutes earlier. 'You may return to your seat.'

I sat down. If my heart was still beating thirteen to the dozen, what must this all be like for Tyler? I looked down at him. The poor kid looked as though he couldn't quite believe what was happening around him. And, looking at his stepmum – out to get him – and his father – silent as the bloody grave, and every bit as chilly – I think I'd find it difficult to believe, too.

Chapter 8

In the end, the whole thing seemed to be over before we knew it, the court having decided that Tyler would be given a 12-month supervision order.

A 'supervision' order meant just that. A youth offending officer would now be assigned to Tyler and would meet up with him regularly – probably on a weekly basis – to hopefully ensure that Tyler understood his 'crime' and would make better choices in the future.

This was good news, at least in terms of the effect it had on Tyler – despite everything, I think a part of him still expected to be 'going down' for ten years – but still felt a bit of a tragedy to me. Only a smallish tragedy in the grand scheme of things – it was hardly heavy handed, given the performance of his stepmother, but at the same time it still seemed out of proportion to the 'crime' given the extent of the background to the actual incident. But it was done now, so I tried not to huff and puff.

Even so, I wasted no time, once Mike had taken Tyler off to the toilets, and Will had gone to fetch his car, to share my thoughts about the outcome with John. I understood Tyler's anxiety about having told me the truth about his stepmother, and how worried he'd been about my sharing what he'd told me with the court, but at the same time, had they really taken everything into consideration? Did they really understand just how difficult a childhood Tyler had had? Was still having – because I didn't see an end to it.

'I know it seems that way, Casey,' John tried to soothe. 'But, honestly, they do have all the same information we have …'

'Not that *I* have,' I pointed out, waggling the rolled-up statement, which would very soon be going into my log. Even if I could only name and shame her there, it would be something.

'Which we do need to talk about, I know,' he said. 'Because it's important.'

He didn't know quite how important yet, though, because we'd not had a chance to even talk about it yet, not really.

'He's made some worrying disclosures, John,' I said.

'I know,' he answered, nodding. 'As you said. But as far as what's happened here is concerned,' he went on, 'a supervision order is probably par for the course. Whatever he's told you – and I don't doubt he's telling the truth – he still took a knife to the woman, and he needs to know what the repercussions of such an action are. And actually, a supervision order is no bad thing for a boy of his age. He's young enough that it might frighten him, rather than antagonise him, which it might if he was older, plus it will give him another confidant, another outlet, another interested adult to whom he can talk about the past – and, hopefully, see his future a little more clearly.'

'Speaking of which,' I said, 'what happens now about resuming contact? From what I've seen – not to mention heard – we're not in the best possible place.'

'I know,' John said again, frowning. But, look, there's Mike and Tyler coming back. Shall I call you later today? Early evening or something? Decide upon some sort of strategy? I have to dash now. Will will be outside – mustn't miss my lift.'

I agreed that was a plan, and then Tyler was back with us again, and someone else seemed to be on his way over – his father.

I nudged Mike. This was the first time we'd seen him or heard him. He wasn't asked to speak in court – another thing that had needled me somewhat; why? – and all we'd seen of him so far was the back of his head.

'Dad!' Tyler called as he approached, running to greet him, while beyond him I could see his wife standing by the coffee machine, holding a paper cup of something and staring right back at me. I gave her a tight smile and turned towards her husband.

'All right, Ty?' he said. I remembered his name was Gareth. He looked to be in his mid-thirties, and was tanned, presumably from working at sea. He leaned forward slightly and gave his son a quick pat on the head. They both had the same mop of dark wavy hair. 'I hope you're being good for Mr and Mrs Watson,' he added, glancing at us. He then held a hand out. Mike shook it and smiled.

'I have, Dad, I promise,' Tyler said, while his father shook my hand. 'When am I coming home now? Will it be soon?'

Incredibly, to my mind, Tyler's father actually glanced back at his wife before answering. Why would he do that? She wasn't even in earshot.

'Not just yet, son,' he said finally, looking profoundly uncomfortable. 'Got to let the dust settle. Let things calm down a bit, yeah? Licia's still a bit shook up by it all.'

I chewed the inside of my cheek to stop myself saying something I might wish I hadn't. *Licia*? There was something about the deferential way he said her name that made me cringe. And definitely something about the whole sorry scenario that made me want to do something more definite than pull a face. This was his child he was talking about. All four foot eleven of him. Hadn't he already just been punished by the court?

And I clearly wasn't the only one who felt rattled. I could almost feel Tyler bristling beside me. He had already followed his father's gaze to the woman who was still standing there, 15 feet away, sipping her drink, observing us.

'But that's not fair!' Tyler blurted out. 'That's not fair, Dad! Just cos she says I stabbed her! And I never – it was an accident! And what about Grant? He wants me home, Dad – who's going to look after him if I'm not there?'

Tyler's dad put a hand on his shoulder. 'Just give it some time, lad,' he repeated. 'We have to think about what's best for everyone, don't we? I've told you, son, Licia's my wife, and I have to do right by her. She's done her best for you, son –'

All this 'son' talk was grating. And not just to me, clearly, because Tyler was having none of it. He wriggled from his father's grasp and put some distance between them, by high-tailing it out of the main doors.

Neither father nor stepmother made any move to follow him. It was Mike who was immediately hot-footing it in pursuit.

Tyler's father looked at me then, with resignation in his eyes. 'What can I do?' his expression said, while his voice provided back-up. 'She's done her best for the lad,' he repeated, as if trying to convince me. 'Brought them up both exactly the same. God only knows how one turns out to be no trouble at all and the other one turns out to be such a wrong 'un. I know it looks bad, Mrs Watson,' he said, almost apologetically, 'but, well. I'm sure you know what happened. His mum was a wrong 'un too, so perhaps it's in his genes …' He tailed off then, glancing back again at his wife, in a gesture that screamed appeasement. A bit like young wolves did when faced with the leader of the pack.

'I do know the background,' was all I could think of to say to him. 'And I'm sure you'll be glad to know that we haven't written him off *just* yet …'

'Oh, of course …' he said, looking embarrassed now. 'But, look, I really have to get off now. I just wanted to come over and introduce myself and let you know how grateful we both are for what you and your husband are doing. Let's hope you can sort him out, eh?' he finished, just as Mike and Tyler were returning, and then, almost as if he wanted to rush away rather than face them, he turned back in the direction of the coffee machine.

To where the she-wolf was waiting, I thought. I couldn't help it; I couldn't see her any other way.

'Come on, love,' I said to Tyler, putting my arm around his shoulder. 'No point hanging around here, is there? Let's jump in the car and go for a burger, eh?'

But Tyler shook his head. He didn't want a burger and neither did he want platitudes. He wanted his dad and his brother and he wanted to go home.

And when was that going to be happening now? Ever?

I glanced at Mike over Tyler's head as we made our way to the car park. *Unlikely*, our eyes said as they met.

It would obviously be unprofessional to stand in judgement over any family in whose lives, as foster carers, we were involved. In the real world, however, that was sometimes easier said than done, because as part of our briefing we sometimes knew too much. And, in our case, given the extreme nature of many of the children's circumstances, what we knew was about family situations that were far from ideal.

Tyler's disclosures to me ate away at me for the rest of the day, and while I had always understood that he had been taken in by his stepmother in extremely difficult circumstances (and that credit must have been due for her selflessness in doing so), what had happened subsequently, from what I could gather from Tyler, anyway, was that she'd done that time-honoured thing of perhaps acting in haste. And it had obviously taken the slog of caring for another woman's child for her to realise she'd made a mistake.

A mistake she now seemed determined to make *him* pay for.

'You don't know that,' Mike had said, reasonably enough, when Tyler was out with Will the following evening, having been picked up by him straight after school. They were off swimming – something Will suggested and to which Tyler had grudgingly agreed, on the basis that there might be a pizza in the equation. We were being lazy as a consequence – sharing a rare Chinese take-away.

'I know I don't,' I admitted, 'but it's so hard to see it any differently. She seems determined to expunge him from their lives, don't you think? And this court situation is a gift.'

'He did pull a knife on her, Case.'

'I know, and I'm never going to condone that. But he maintains that he never meant to stab her and I believe him. Just like I believe what he says about her systematic cruelty. God, Mike, isn't it cruel enough that he wasn't even allowed to call her "Mum"? Can you imagine how that must have eaten away at him? He was three, and it was made clear that he and Grant were not even *remotely* equal. That's extreme mental cruelty right there!'

'I know, love,' Mike said again. 'But –'

'And what about his father?' I said, pushing my plate away irritably. 'What did you make of him? How could he stand there and say what he said in all conscience?'

'Because he's weak? Because he's piggy in the middle?'

'Exactly,' I said. 'You've hit the nail on the head. I know it might not be that simple, but it doesn't seem that complicated, either. She's the one calling the shots and her ultimatum's clear. Tyler or her. And, of course, he doesn't know the half of it, does he? That's why I'm so ambivalent about Tyler's disclosures not being read out in court.'

'But do you really think it would have made any difference? They had one job to do – try an assault case against a juvenile – and they did that. Would knowing he's had a rubbish start in life have changed the outcome?'

'Possibly not, but now it's so obvious she's determined to be shot of him anyway, it would have been good to let that particular cat out of the bag, and let the court – *and* his father – know what's been going on in his absence.'

Mike shook his head. 'Yes, but how do you know he *doesn't* know? I know Tyler chooses to believe she's telling lies to his dad about him, but you know how these things work – what's to say he isn't all too aware? Just chooses to turn a blind eye so as not to upset the apple cart?'

'So you think he's in on it?'

'He could well be. And even if he's not, he could still be quietly condoning it – putting his head in the sand rather than risk confrontation. But love,' he added gently, 'what can we do about any of it anyway? It may well be that he doesn't love Tyler either – let's face it, it's been known. He didn't bond with him as a baby, did he? Just got handed him and told, "Here you are – these are your genes, mate." And if they don't love him, either of them – which *is* how I see it, to be honest, however much of a show Dad puts on

– then of course they don't want to take care of him, so what's the point in even dwelling on it? If that's the case, surely the best thing is to stop flogging a dead horse. That's the reality of the situation, is it not?'

It was chilling to hear it but, of course, he was right. Which was what made it all so depressing. No matter how hard we worked on Tyler, how much time we all spent helping him fight his demons and move forward, what he might be moving on to might be the loss of such family as he had – the little brother he so obviously loved, and I felt sure loved him. How in all conscience could we let that happen?

'We're not going to,' said John, the following morning, when he was finally able to pop round and talk things through. I'd already emailed him my statement, together with an up-to-date copy of my usual log, so between them he had the clearest picture to date of both how things had been with Tyler since he'd come to us, and how life had been up to the point of the knife incident.

It was the last day of the summer term today and, as of that afternoon, we'd have six weeks of long days to fill with our young charge – the key thing being to keep him out of mischief. For which I already had a few plans – doing some gardening for my mum and dad being one of them, joining Kieron's footie crew being another – but it was a lot of space to fill.

But John had said what he'd said with an air of conviction. Which was encouraging. 'Have you got a plan, then?' I wanted to know.

'Sort of,' he said, 'though not a hard and fast one. We thought we'd leave it a couple of weeks then see if we could fix up a meeting with the Broughtons. Now the court hearing is behind us, the plan was – and still is, up to a point – to see if we can open up a dialogue. See if there's potential to have some sort of organised contact with his brother, and perhaps his dad, with, if at all possible, a view to him *perhaps* eventually returning home.'

I put down my coffee mug. I had picked up on something. '"Was, and still is, up to a point"?' I asked him.

He grinned at me. 'Trust you to spot that, Casey!' But the grin soon turned to a worried sigh. 'The truth is that Tyler's disclosures have added a new aspect to things, haven't they? If what he's said is true then there are obviously issues we can't ignore. We can't un-know things we now know, can we?'

He made a good point. One of Tyler's disclosures had been that his stepmother was actively abusing him – or at least being extremely physical in her punishments. He'd also confessed to stealing on her behalf, and being sworn to secrecy on pain of more beatings; if proven, things like that simply couldn't be ignored. 'So what's the next step?' I asked.

'Well, we still want to speak to the family; at the very least, his father. It's clear Tyler has a strong bond with his brother, and is keen to have a relationship with his dad. So whatever the situation with the stepmother we have a duty – if appropriate – to foster a resumption of relations there. As to how far that takes us …' he shrugged. 'Who knows, Casey? The bottom line is that if they don't want him back, we can't push it. Only try to make them appreciate Tyler's position.'

'Which is that the poor little sod's between a rock and a hard place,' I said.

'I know,' John said, 'I know – 'twas ever thus, eh?'

He was right there. There wasn't a child that came our way that wasn't in some awful bind or other. Whether they'd been neglected or abused, beaten or just brow-beaten, pushed from pillar to post in care, or within chaotic unhappy families, the one thing that bound them was the thing that always got my goat – that none of it was ever their fault. Yes, you could point the finger towards bad actions, bad behaviours and bad attitudes, and the older a child got, the more inclined society was to do that. But the truth was that almost all of the time there was a common, depressing truth – that they had been let down pretty badly in some way or other, and everything that followed was generally a result of that.

It mattered not a jot to me that these parents – well, parent and step-parent – felt aggrieved to have had to take on that motherless three-year-old. No, perhaps it wasn't fair, wasn't part of their plan. But they *had* done so, sealing his fate. Which might have been different. If he'd been fostered as a three-year-old, he might have been adopted instead, mightn't he? By adoptive parents who would probably have cherished him. Instead, he was more or less orphaned as an 11-year-old, and, crucially, having already formed a bond with what he'd thought was his family. Which made it *so* much worse.

'God, you said it, John,' I agreed.

Chapter 9

I began the start of the summer holidays determined to keep positive. Nothing was set in stone, and perhaps John was right. Perhaps once he gave some thought to what had happened, Tyler's father *would* make some sort of effort to try and re-integrate his elder son into his family – even if it was out of guilt rather than parental love. We could only hope. And perhaps Alicia (or the faintly icky 'Licia', as he'd called her) would feel shamed into making some sort of effort towards reconciliation, too.

No, it wasn't likely to be perfect, but what mattered most was that the connection wasn't broken, because that connection was key to Tyler seeing his brother, and that really mattered. However dysfunctional Tyler's family set-up, his relationship with his brother was something pure and good and must not under any circumstances be allowed to flounder. I felt that as strongly as I'd felt anything, ever. Whatever happened with the rest of it, that was the vital link. It was a bond that could mean the difference between Tyler thriving and losing it. Something he could take through life with him, whatever else happened. That there was someone in the world who loved him unconditionally.

If I felt tearful even thinking that, I definitely felt on the edge of blubbering as Tyler tried to adjust to his new reality over the next few days. We tried hard to keep him busy and positive, but it hung over him like a veil, and I knew that encounter outside the courtroom had really crushed him. And that wasn't surprising, was it? It had been the first time he'd seen his dad since he'd been placed with us, and his dad couldn't have made it plainer that not only was he not that fussed about seeing Tyler, he was without question putting his wife's 'needs' first.

I was therefore constantly trying to put a positive spin on everything, pointing out that things might well change once the dust had settled, that John was working towards them getting together, that he might soon see Grant, but at the same time I didn't want to go overboard with that theme as, in reality, it might not be happening. Tyler, too, tried his best to stay hopeful. Like all children, all he wanted was to be loved by those he cared for, and to entertain the possibility that his love for his dad might not be reciprocated was anathema – it probably just wouldn't compute.

I'd seen that, too, many times, and it never got any easier. With our first foster child, Justin – he'd been so desperate for any tiny shred of affection from a mother who had spent all 11 years of his young life demonstrating that there was none. He'd been in and out of care since he was five when he'd come to us – and, most of the time, it had been her who'd made the call to have him taken. Yet still he hoped, because children are hard-wired to hope, despite the mountain of evidence that, actually, hope was pointless – that she'd rather be shot of her eldest child altogether.

We still saw Justin regularly – he was 17 now – and nothing had changed. Still he tried to make overtures, still she brusquely rebuffed them, and he'd be back licking his wounds before trying again.

Then there were the children who'd come to us looking like Dickensian urchins, having suffered both an unspeakable level of neglect and systematic sexual abuse. They still loved the grandad who had committed such evil; still craved cuddles with that vile human monster. Still loved the mother who'd stood by and allowed it to happen. It was sick but it was also a fact of life.

I obviously couldn't make Tyler's dad love him and stand by him, but I could at least show him that there were people in the world who cared for him, and during the first couple of weeks of the school holidays I kept him on a tight leash with his points and kept him busy. He went to football with Kieron on the Saturday – without incident – and the following Tuesday I took him round to spend the afternoon at Mum and Dad's.

'It will be a great opportunity for you to earn yourself some points,' I told him. 'Points you need if you're going to get any more credit on that phone of yours.'

Since having his wings clipped by the court, Tyler's behaviour had been generally acceptable at home, but he was still prone to bouts of disobedience. Once he got in that 'the world hates me so I hate the world' mood, trying to get him to do as he was told was like trying to push a car up a hill through treacle.

But the relentless warmth-assault from all of us was hard to resist, and with my mum and dad growing so fond of him, he'd been round there again. I'd since taken him twice more, the first time with Riley and the little ones, where he seemed to really enjoy playing with Levi and Jackson. He was a typical older brother, naturally assuming the role of head honcho – which, given the boisterous boy-games he naturally wanted to organise, Levi and Jackson lapped up with great enthusiasm. I also took him round a couple of days later, to help me mow the lawn and weed the garden – and, again, he rose to the challenge with a gratifying amount of gusto, particularly when I trusted him to manage the elderly Flymo on his own.

He also had a session with the court-appointed officer, a rather stuffy 40-something man called Mr Jonathon Smart – with emphasis very much on the 'mister' and the 'smart'. He was meant to be doing some reparation work with Tyler, using a variety of media methods, such as art work, clay modelling and writing letters to victims. Although in Tyler's case it was deemed unnecessary to have to write to his stepmum if he didn't want to – in the interests of maintaining family harmony. *Family harmony, my foot!* I thought when Mr Smart mentioned this to me. He clearly had little idea of the family dynamic. And not much more about making a connection with 11-year-old boys, to my mind. But I held my tongue. He was only doing what he'd been appointed to, after all, and the charitable side of me felt bound not to stand in judgement. Even so, it all still felt like a case of going through the motions.

The sessions were held in my living room, and while they were happening I was expected to make myself scarce. This suited me just fine, as his old-fashioned, out-of-touch manner set my teeth on edge, and I much preferred to have the chance to harness my irritation by launching into productive bouts of even-more-frenetic-that-usual cleaning.

It was to be the following Wednesday, however, when it really hit home that, while all the activities did a great job of filling the days with positives (well, perhaps bar the Mr Smart sessions), what Tyler needed more than anything was some connection with his *own* family – specifically, some quality time with his younger brother. It just wasn't right or natural for them to be parted like this.

Will had taken Tyler swimming again, and the reason for his enthusiasm for the sport was now apparent – Will's younger brother was a lifeguard at the local leisure pool and he often took his young charges there. They'd gone off at around three and I'd been expecting them back at six-ish, but a text from Will at around five had alerted me to the fact that they probably wouldn't return home till after seven.

And the reason why became apparent as soon as they arrived back. Usually, Will would drop him off and we'd wave goodbye from the doorstep, but tonight, as Tyler thundered up the path, swimming bag swinging madly from his shoulder, I noticed Will was climbing out of the car as well.

'I've been to a party!' Tyler exclaimed. 'Look!' he said, thrusting a small bag towards me. 'I've got a lump of cake and everything!'

To see such a smile on his face was a lovely, lovely thing. 'A party?' I said, as Will headed towards us. 'How lovely. Whose party was this?'

'It was Grant's friend. He's called Daniel, and he was 11, and he was having a swimming party. They had the big inflatable out and everything. It was epic!'

Will, too, was grinning. 'He blagged an invite, didn't you, Ty? Charm the birds out of the trees, this one,' he said, chuckling.

'I didn't blag it!' Tyler corrected indignantly. 'It was Dan's mum – she just invited me. Will told her who I was an' that I was Grant's brother and everything, and she said I could join in. And our team won the relay race, so I got a bunch of sweets as well!'

He was like a bottle of pop, he was so excited, and I felt a rush of love for him. He'd had a rubbish few weeks, all told – excluded from his last school, thrown into a new one where he knew no one, the court case, the reality of his fractured, broken family. Thank heavens for Daniel's mum. Whoever she was, I could have hugged her. Bless her for showing him such kindness.

'Sweets as well?' I said. 'Yum. I hope you've saved a couple for me.'

'You can have them all,' he said, thrusting the bag towards me. 'Well, what's left in there anyway. I'm stuffed. We had, like, *so* much food, Casey. It was like a feast! And guess what?'

'What?' I laughed.

'There's brilliant news, isn't there, Will?'

Will nodded and smiled, but as he looked at me I saw something else cross his eyes. A hint of reticence?

'It's about Grant,' Tyler said. 'He's only coming to my school, Casey!'

'Is that so?' I said, feigning surprise. 'Well, I never!'

'Isn't that *brilliant*? He starts in September. So we'll be able to see each other all the time in school and everything.'

'That would indeed be brilliant,' I agreed. 'Something to look forward to,' I added. 'Though right now you need to get those wet things out and hung up, don't you? Actually, I tell you what – why don't you pop them straight in the washing machine so I can give them a rinse? And what d'you say?' I added, as he made to head inside.

'Oh, yeah, sorry. Thanks a mill, Will!' he said, as they high-fived. 'See you next week, yeah?'

'You bet, kiddo,' said Will, ruffling his hair.

'Thanks a mill, Will?' I said, laughing as Tyler trotted off into the kitchen.

Will grinned. 'It's kind of become our thing,' he explained. 'His idea. Phew – quite an afternoon in the end, that one.'

'And no sign of stepmother?'

'No, thank God. Well, on balance – after your run-in with her. I think Grant was being dropped home by one of the other mums. He's had such a good time, Casey. It was such a tonic for him to do something like that.'

'I'll bet,' I said. 'Whoever that woman is, she deserves a hug and a medal.'

'It was a lovely gesture, wasn't it? And it was so good for him to be able to spend a bit of time with his brother – honestly, he was like a different kid. We really do have to find a way to get some contact set up there.'

'You're telling me,' I said. 'For *both* of their sakes.'

'And speaking of birthday parties, have you thought about Tyler's at all? Only he mentioned that his is just after they go back to school. And, of course, now he's talking about having a pool party of some sort. Not on that kind of scale, of course – Christ, the poor kid's hardly had a chance to make any school friends yet, has he? But I thought I'd mention it as something we could perhaps think about.'

'Yes, of course,' I agreed. I hadn't actually given it a thought yet – though I'd filed his date of birth in my head early on in the process (it was one of those things I tended to do automatically) it had completely slipped my mind that it was coming up so soon. 'And, yes,' I added, 'I don't see why we couldn't do something like that. And we're like rent-a-crowd, us Watsons, so no problems with numbers. And I'm sure there must be a couple of friends from his old school that we could see about inviting. There's definitely that older boy – Cameron? And I'm sure there are a couple more. He's on that mobile enough, for sure. Well, when he's earned enough credit.'

'Good,' Will said decisively. 'So that's something for us to mull. And I'm sure my bro would be able to sort something out for us. But right now I'll leave you to it …'

'I will duly mull,' I said, feeling more positive than I had since the court appearance. And even more determined to press for some contact with Grant. 'I think that's a brilliant idea,' I agreed as he turned to go. 'Oh, and – one more thing …'

'I know,' he said, turning back and rolling his eyes. 'Thanks a mill, Will, by any chance?'

I liked Will, I decided. Very much. Mr Smart could definitely learn from him. Team Tyler was shaping up very well.

Chapter 10

Over the next couple of days I felt happier than I had about Tyler since he'd come to us. Happy that the court case was behind us, happy that he was forging a great relationship with his social worker, happy that we would surely find a path through the acrimony and get something set up whereby he could have regular contact with his little brother. Happy, all in all, that we could make some progress.

I also felt happy that Tyler was going to have his brother in school with him come September, because it had made such a difference to his mood. How could I not find that a positive? But the truth was that, although I tried not to show it, I was at the same time a bit on edge about it, too. That fate had conspired to place them in the same high school was out of our hands – and in some ways it was a welcome development. But another part of me, looking into less positive scenarios, had started having niggling, persistent concerns. I said as much to John when he next phoned for an update.

'What if this family reconciliation doesn't come about?' I said once I'd filled him in on the latest developments. 'In that circumstance, won't it just serve to drive home the fact that Grant is with the family, and Tyler isn't?'

'I know,' John said, 'but there's little we can do about it either way, is there? And let's try to remain positive. Our aim for Tyler was always to reconcile him with Alicia and Gareth. And, all the revelations notwithstanding, that's still one of several possible outcomes, isn't it?'

I wasn't sure I agreed. The more I thought about it, the more I worried that he might end up being returned to a place of cruelty, not acceptance. 'What, even after all the things she's done and said to him, John? After all the things he's told us?'

Though even as I asked it, I knew the answer. Much as I knew John shared my concerns about Alicia's fitness to parent Tyler, I also knew that if there was any slim hope of Alicia shaping up and having a change of heart, then social services would cling to this and attempt to make it so. They'd work on the basis that she could change her ways. Be given support. Learn, if not to cherish him, at least to give him the bare minimum of parenting – which, almost all of the time, was better than being in care. So it was absolutely the right thing to do, and much as it upset me I knew they were right.

'I know, I know,' I said, 'and I realise we'd have to give it a chance. But my number one aim is to push for contact with Grant. Formal contact, so that when they return to school it's not a case of them "bumping into" each other and having clandestine meetings – that it's a normal part of official contact that's already in place. I know that's going to be a sticking point, given the bloody hoo-hah we had in the supermarket, but hopefully his father will see it as reasonable and make her agree to it – you know, proper supervised family time – all of them together.'

'Exactly what I was thinking, Casey. And I am mindful of your concerns about our Mrs Broughton, too. In fact, I've already spoken to Will about it, and our plan is to go and see the pair of them, at home together. I'm pretty sure that, between us, we'll be able to get a sense of the true lie of the land.'

'That's great,' I said, relieved that John intended to investigate further before making a decision. Because we didn't live in la-la land, and what we now knew about some of the cruelties Alicia had inflicted on Tyler couldn't, as John had said, now be un-known. 'Will you let me know as soon as you can?' I asked him. 'I'm already having to watch what I say so that I don't give him any false hope – so it would be good to have a clearer idea of what we need to prepare him for, wouldn't it?'

I sat tight, waiting on John, for well over a fortnight, Tyler's father having apparently gone back to his oil rig for his next stint; and there was no way John and Will were going to go round till he was home again. In the meantime, the school holidays ended and Tyler returned to school – and, of course, was now regularly seeing his little brother.

And it seemed he was settling into year 8 very positively. I didn't know if it was the Grant effect, the Will effect, or even the Mr Smart effect – it could have been a combination, or just that he was adapting to his new situation, but I had a call from his new head of year at the end of his first week to let me know how pleased she was with his behaviour.

There was a knock-on effect at home too. Tyler had raced through the programme he'd been doing at home with me and Mike, and was now nearing the end of level two. This meant he had a lot more flexibility in the home, and also more freedom to choose what he did with his spare time. And the fact that Tyler realised this himself, and was feeling the benefits, was brought home to me just a couple of days into the second week of term. He had started walking home by this point and came charging through the door.

'Casey, guess what!' he yelled, dropping his coat and bag on the hall floor before running towards me. 'Our Grant said that your link thingy man is off round to Dad's tonight. Will's going too, he thinks, and Grant thinks it's about me moving back home! Can you believe it? So Alicia must be sorry by now, mustn't she?'

The words had come out in an excitable tumble. I smiled, but at the same time I felt anxious about his complete confidence that this was it – that he was definitely heading home.

'That's good news,' I said carefully, 'but we mustn't count our chickens, love. We don't know *for sure* that's why they're going round, do we?'

But he was not to be corrected. 'But it must be – Grant heard them whispering about it. An' the only thing it *can* be about is me. Didn't no one tell you about it?' he added, obviously beginning to wonder about that.

'No,' I lied, 'but, love, like I said, we can't jump to conclusions, can we? It might be just that they're going round there to tell them how good you've been lately and how …'

'Yes!' Tyler interrupted. 'Course! Might be that, mightn't it? And that's fine too, because when they hear they're going to want me back for sure.' He gave me such a lovely smile then, before turning to deal with his coat and bag, as per the house rules. 'See? You've done a good job with me, Casey,' he said, hanging his coat on its hook. 'You and Mike, and that. They're going to be *well* pleased. They'll know I'm not a bad lad any more. I'll tell 'em that you and Mike don't do drugs or anything, too, so they'll know it's not in me any more.'

And with that, he ran upstairs to his room to get changed, while I reflected wryly on our getting that clean bill of health. I then went into the living room to call John, ostensibly to let him know that Tyler had already heard all about it, though, in truth, it was more of a knee-jerk than anything – it wouldn't make any difference to anything, after all. I just wanted to connect; see if there was anything else I didn't know.

But I was obviously too late. John's office phone went straight to voicemail, and there didn't seem much sense in calling him on his mobile; he and Will might even be *en route* there right then. No, all I could usefully do was wait. And start fretting.

Happily, Kieron phoned soon after – just for a chat, as far as he'd thought, anyway – so I cajoled him into popping round for a bit. Tyler was somewhat over-excited, and instinct told me that the best thing would be for him to have both a distraction and a bit of physical exercise. So we dug out a football and Kieron took Tyler over to the park for an hour, so they could work on his goal-scoring skills. And I was also grateful because I was on such pins about what was happening that I knew it would end up transmitting to Tyler, and that was the last thing we wanted. No, there was nothing to be done but wait for John's phone call and cross everything crossable for good news.

'But still prepare for the possibility of bad news,' Mike cautioned, as he helped me prepare a salad to go with the pasta bake I'd made.

'I know, love,' I said. 'That's what's killing me. I'm not sure we shouldn't actually prepare him for bad news maybe – you know, as in tonight; lay the groundwork, temper his expectations a little more.'

But Mike shook his head. 'You know, Case, we'll have to deal with what we'll have to deal with. I think we should leave that to John and Will, don't you? If the outcome is negative then I think it's better if they're the ones that tell him. We shouldn't be the bearers of bad news all the time, should we? Our job is to deal with the fall-out, yes, but only after *they* impart the news.'

Mike was right. I should probably stop second-guessing

the outcome, and I should definitely leave the telling of it in John's experienced hands, and in the meantime try not to think about something I could do absolutely nothing to influence. It could be the best news, it could be the worst news – or it could be somewhere in between. In life, I found, things usually were.

Of course, it was impossible not to think about what might have happened at that meeting. Would Dad have stepped up and put his son's case to his wife? Would they see reason *re* contact with Grant? Would they agree to some sort of supervised family contact? But however many scenarios I pictured as I lay awake that night, I never imagined the one I was presented with the next day. It was a Thursday morning, which meant double PE for Tyler and a guarantee that he'd leave the house in a good mood. Which I tried to match, though I still felt a sharp pang of guilt as I watched him sprint off down the path, grinning widely, a slice of toast still in his hand.

I loved that he seemed so much happier generally, that he'd seemed to make friends – friends he could meet on the corner – that, in one area of his life, at least, things were calming down. But at the same time I felt the weight of the 'what-ifs' bearing down on me, hoping that he wouldn't soon be taking a step back. But that weight was completely natural – life had a habit of doing that, didn't it? Of throwing a spanner in the works from time to time.

It was 10.00 a.m. by the time the phone went, and I almost lunged at it.

'Oh, thank goodness,' I said when I realised who it was. 'I tried to reach you last night, actually, but you'd obviously set off to the Broughton's ...'

'You knew that?' John said.

'Yes, I did. Tyler told me.' I quickly filled John in on Tyler's excited announcement the previous day. 'So please tell me the meeting went well,' I pleaded. 'I've been worrying like mad, as you can imagine.'

'Oh, Casey,' John said, with a sigh in his voice. An unmistakable harbinger of doom. 'I'm afraid it didn't,' he said. 'No point in beating about the bush here. Listen, my plan is to drive over to you as soon as I've caught up with my manager. That okay? I shouldn't be more than an hour. Probably less.'

'But can't you just tell me now?' I asked. I was irritated now and just wanted to know. But no. He said it would be better if he explained everything in person and that he'd be there just as soon as he could.

I'd just have to wait. There was nothing else for it. So I used the time positively – as much for me as for Tyler – and went on the local leisure centre website to research their parties and how to book them, for his upcoming birthday. What did Mary Poppins say? (As if I even needed reminding.) That a spoonful of sugar always helped the medicine go down? And though there wasn't much I could do about whatever gloomy news John had for me, I could at least have something positive to sweeten the pill.

And it turned out I would be desperately in need of something positive, as almost as soon as I'd ushered John into the kitchen and given him a coffee he made his pronouncement – that it had basically been 'bloody awful'.

'They know all about the boys seeing each other at school,' John explained, 'and they basically want Will to put a stop to it. Just like that – as if we can just wave a wand and make it happen!'

'Did they give a reason?' I wanted to know, anxious to hear on what grounds they were making this insane demand – after all, what did they think social services could organise? That Grant spend the rest of his life wrapped in a Tyler-deflecting force-field?

'Oh, yes,' he said. 'They had one ready. They said seeing Tyler was upsetting Grant; that it had made him "aggressive" when he got home from school. In fact they went as far as to say they were considering taking Grant out of the school if things didn't improve. So I tried to reason with them – pointing out that, surely, the boys seeing each other was a positive –'

'Which it so obviously is!' I said indignantly.

'Exactly,' John agreed. 'And for both boys. I pointed out that *both* were doing well in their respective classes, both academically and socially, and that's when it all got a bit, um, messy.'

'Messy?' I parroted, wondering at his unusual choice of word.

'Yes, messy,' he said. 'They obviously didn't want to hear anything we were saying, and when Will pointed out that it would be crucial to Tyler's well-being to have some contact with his sibling, we got a barrage of counter-fire, mostly from Mrs Broughton, as you'd expect, about how

Tyler's well-being – and there might have been some reference to his "druggy" mother – wasn't coming at the cost of her own mental health or being achieved at the expense of her own son. I'm sure you can picture the scene …'

I could, too. All too readily. 'That bad, eh?'

He nodded. 'Worse, actually. Because when I dared to use the term "parental responsibility", in relation to Tyler's *father's* responsibility, we were treated to another blast of "Who do you think you are, interfering and telling us what to do?" And various rants about home-wrecking kids practically being dumped on them by social services, etc., etc., and, yes, sadly, Dad was joining in too.'

'Unbelievable,' I said shaking my head. 'I just can't get my head round it. Her, yes, but how can that man just disown his flesh and blood like that?'

'*Really*, Casey?' John asked, though it wasn't a question. 'You *really* need me to tell you that?'

And, of course, he didn't need to. Why else was the care system straining under the pressure and bursting at the seams? Because of all the children like Tyler in the world.

'And I think she's been working on him, to be honest,' John went on. 'Will and I both do. This whole business of things negatively impacting on *her* son – it doesn't ring true to us, and I doubt it does to you. But as to what to do now – well, the bottom line is that we were told to "f" off – *literally*. Oh, and, rather charmingly, that we could "stick Tyler up our arses". And then we were pretty much manhandled out of the bloody door.'

'But he was so apologetic in court!' I bleated.

'Window dressing,' John corrected. 'He dances to her tune, Casey. He's been given a choice, and he seems to have made it.'

'So that's that?'

He sighed. 'I'm afraid so. For the present, anyway. We'll be looking at a long-term foster home now, obviously. So the fact that the lad's doing well at his points is something to be grateful for, at least.'

'*Has* been,' I said. 'John, you know that could all change now.'

'I know,' he said, 'but let's not be hitting him with any bombshells. My plan is to let things settle and then re-address the business of the brothers seeing each other at least – perhaps if we don't press for family reconciliation, they might be persuaded to give ground *re* the boys. I don't know, Casey,' he said, 'but let's play it on a day-to-day basis for now.'

'So don't tell him, basically.'

'No, not yet. Don't spell it out. Keep it positive but tempered. Let's see how things go. You know, "Keep up the good work in school" – that kind of thing.'

And you'll be rewarded by – what? I thought, miserably. *Rejection anyway*. I sat in silence for a few seconds, trying to take it all in. What kind of people were we dealing with here? But the truth was that, tragically, we were dealing with pretty much the kind of people we usually dealt with – or rather didn't. That was probably key. Because most of the time all we knew of the places our foster kids had come from was that they were bad places, places where no child should be, and certainly nowhere you'd ever want them to go back to.

I should have *known* that – known it the minute I was summoned to the police station. Instead, because there *was* a family, *was* a dad, *was* a brother, I'd practised my default position of misplaced optimism and hope.

And I shouldn't have. Guilty as charged.

Chapter 11

To say that Tyler took the news badly was something of an understatement – even in response to the heavily edited version I'd decided to give him, following John's directive not to completely dash his hopes.

'You mean it wasn't even about me going home?' he demanded when I tried to explain that it was more of a progress report, really.

'Not really, sweetie,' I told him gently. 'They just went round for a chat. That's how things are done – just giving them an update, you know, to see how everyone's feeling –'

'Well, I'm feeling *horrible*,' he said, digging an angry fist into each hip. 'An' no one ever asked me how *I'm* feeling, did they?'

'I know, love,' I said, sensing from his body language that this wasn't the moment to try and give him a cuddle. He was too angry, too stiff, too appalled. 'But I'm sure things will get sorted out soon,' I tried to soothe, 'and, hey, next week's your birthday – how about we think about that instead, eh? Have you given any thought to what you'd like to do? How about that pool party we were talking about? Shall we have Will see what he can do for us? Only I've been looking on the internet and –'

'I don't *care* about my fucking stupid *birthday*!' he yelled, the explosion of rage we'd mostly kept below a simmer for a good few weeks now bursting out of him. 'That horrible witch has done for me!' he spat. 'I know she has! She *always* does! She's told my dad I'm a pile of *shit*, otherwise I'd be home now, wouldn't I? I fucking hate *both* of them!' With which he turned on his heel and thundered up the stairs.

I stood there, slightly shocked, as his bedroom door slammed. And so hard it almost rattled out all my fillings. Then I was shocked at the business of *being* shocked. How could I have forgotten just how angry he could get?

I felt angry too. How else would he be expected to feel, frankly? He'd been abandoned and vilified and, however I tried to dress it up, he knew it. How could apparently normal adults care so little for the emotional damage they inflicted on children they were supposed to be taking care of? How could they be so cruelly resistant to the idea of giving – even just a little? How could they be so cold and hostile and sleep at night? I turned and followed Tyler up the stairs, knowing just how little I could say to make things better for him. Of course he was angry. I was bloody angry, too.

Luckily, we'd now hit the weekend. Which was a blessing, because though there wasn't much I could do while Tyler adjusted to this new reality, what I could do was rally the troops. It wasn't a universal panacea – for some kids, in some situations, it was the last thing I would have considered – but in this situation, with this newly distraught little boy, I sensed that I'd need the whole family to help get us through. So on the Saturday morning I invited Riley, David and the kids round for Sunday lunch, along with Kieron and Lauren, who'd been planning on coming anyway, and my mum and dad, to give them a break from cooking.

'I just want to take Tyler's mind off the situation at home for a bit,' I explained to Riley – not that Riley needed any encouragement to agree to having someone else cook the roast – 'and try to get him excited about his birthday while we're at it. Right now, as far as he's concerned, there's not going to *be* a birthday. I haven't a clue what to get him, much less think about planning a party.'

'Oh, don't you worry,' Riley reassured me, 'the boys'll soon cheer him up. And I'll put Levi on a secret mission to find out what he'd most like. Course, he'll probably come back with a long list of nonsense, but at least he'll be distracted. That's the main thing.'

I hoped she was right, though the signs weren't encouraging when I went up to explain to Tyler the following morning that the whole family were descending in a couple of hours. 'Well, they'd better not come up here and touch any of my stuff,' he warned. 'And I don't want to have to listen to that baby wailing all day, neither.'

'Oh, for goodness sake, Tyler,' I said mildly, 'Marley-Mae is just a baby. That's how they communicate – you know that. What else are they supposed to do? When you feel bad you can tell someone – Marley Mae can't do that.'

I paused then, wondering if it might be a good moment to suggest that a problem shared is a problem brought down to more manageable proportions. Since his short rant the previous day, he had clammed up completely, withdrawing into himself and refusing to venture out again. Mike and I had both tried, but he was resolutely in 'I don't want to talk about it' mode now, and I knew there was no point in pressuring him till he was ready. So instead, I tutted. 'Anyway, stop being a grump,' I said. 'You'll enjoy it. In fact, why don't you plan something you boys can all do, before they get here? Like make a big den, perhaps – you could make one in the garden, if you like. A great big one – they'd love that – and you could plan a game for it, too.'

Tyler rolled his eyes and pointedly picked up his football comic. 'I don't want to,' he said, 'and you can't make me. They're just *babies*. And I don't *want* to play with babies. I want *Grant*,' he railed then, suddenly animated, and throwing down the comic he'd just picked up. 'If Grant was here we'd have *proper* fun, not have to play *baby* games!'

'Yes, well,' I said, conscious that he was trying to work us both up to another rant-fest, 'you'll see Grant in school tomorrow and you can have some fun then. In the meantime stop looking for excuses not to be happy, and come down and have some toast or something before they get here.'

'God,' he huffed. 'Do I *have* to?'

'Yes, you absolutely have to,' I said firmly.

* * *

It's never easy keeping a smile glued in place in the face of constant negativity, but I was determined to keep things relentlessly upbeat, even if it did mean I had jaw-ache by the end of the day. It seemed the only thing to do, in any case. There was very little we could do about Tyler's situation, no, but what I knew we could do was give him something else to focus on – at least till such time as he felt able to sit down and process what his new future might hold.

It was a beautiful late summer day, and we spent almost all of it in the garden. I'd set up the garden dining furniture so that we could have our lunch al fresco and, as Tyler had shown no enthusiasm for my den-building idea, put out all the garden toys, including the giant Jenga and skittles.

Not that it was a pleasing scene of riotous outdoor fun. As I prepared lunch, chatting to Riley and Lauren in the kitchen – and, of course, gurgling at Marley Mae – the men were all in the living room watching some crucial football programme, Levi built up Jenga blocks and Jackson bounced on the trampoline, while Tyler watched from the sidelines, his hood over his head and a scowl on his face.

'He's worn it all day,' I told Lauren when she commented on his black mood.

'What, the hoodie or the frown?' Riley said.

'Both,' I said. I knocked on the window, then, and opened it. 'Tyler, go on, love,' I said. 'Why don't you help Levi with the Jenga?' and though he stood up and mooched over (he wasn't stupid; he had lots of 'being helpful' points to earn if he wanted to keep his phone topped up) it was with about as much enthusiasm as if I'd asked him to put the bins out.

'You know, I'd just leave him, Casey,' Lauren said. 'Let him wallow for a bit, feel sorry for himself. He's a bright boy – he knows it's not your fault he can't go home. So sooner or later he's bound to stop taking it out on you.'

Riley agreed, and perhaps they were both right. Keen as I was to keep up the assault of cheeriness and positivity, perhaps I should just let him withdraw a bit to lick his wounds.

For a bit, anyway. One thing I wasn't going to allow to happen was for his birthday to pass under a cloud of misery – not on my watch. Given all I'd seen and heard of his family, I imagined no one had ever made much of a fuss of him on his birthday, and, if it was within my power, I was determined to break the cycle. However feeble the effort they made (and I didn't doubt they would do very little more than observe the usual niceties), I could at least do that for him – give him a bunch of happy birthday memories to take away with him.

Course, it never occurred to me just how wrong I could be.

Dinner that day was a rowdy affair, what with so many of us crammed round my six-seater garden table, on various battered and different-sized chairs. But at least Tyler had, by that time, thawed slightly. He seemed happy to get involved with the boys' usual gross jokes about their food, even laughing as Levi told him how sweetcorn always came out in his poo. Which was a touch rank, but at least helped ease the tension. And having roped in as many of the family as I could (Mike would have to be at work, sadly) I also felt more confident that by the time his birthday party came around the following Thursday he would be in the right frame of mind to enjoy it.

He certainly responded positively when I told him about it that evening. 'Oh, my *God*!' he raved, when I handed him some blank invitations. 'You mean it? I can *really* have my own pool party? That's epic! Oh my *God*!'

'Yes, of course I mean it,' I laughed. 'All organised for after school this Thursday. All you need to do is decide which of your friends you'd like to invite. We can't manage a whole classful, I'm afraid – too short notice. But if you can choose half a dozen friends, that would be fine. Your friend Cameron, too,' I added. 'If you'd like to.'

I'd agonised a little about that, what with him apparently being 15, but, right now, Tyler needed all the friends he could get. And this Cameron was clearly important in his life.

'Oh my *God*,' he said again. Perhaps I needed to pull him up on that – but not today. '*Can* I? He'd be made up! God, this will be *great*. And with the big inflatable and everything?' I nodded. '*Wowww*. This'll be my best *ever* party, *ever*. O.M.G. – just you wait till I tell Grant!'

Though this likelihood hadn't escaped me, I still had to think on my feet. 'That's my plan,' I said, smiling at him, 'and I'm sure Grant would love to come. Though you might need to bear in mind that he might have something on already. I think I remember John mentioning something he might be doing this week when we talked about it … just to warn you. You know, in case. You know how things are – it's all a bit short-notice, isn't it? What with us just having had the summer holidays and everything …'

And I'd obviously kept it light enough to do the trick.

'Oh, well,' he said, flapping a dismissive hand, 'if he can't come he can't come. Bet he will, though.' He chuckled. 'Like, *doh* – he wouldn't want to cancel whatever he was doing?! He will so want to come. Oh, this is *epic*!'

I called John as soon as Tyler had left for school the following morning. Much as I was cheered by the turnaround in his mood by the end of the weekend, I was now really anxious that Grant not being allowed to go to his party would plunge him straight back to square one.

'So I was wondering if you could do a bit more of your "interfering busybody from social services" act, and, if they're dead set on refusing to allow Grant to go – which I'm assuming they will be – could they at least make an excuse or something about why?'

'I can try,' John said. 'But the bottom line is that they'll do what they like, won't they? But look on the bright side: Tyler's not stupid – he'll know where it's coming from. He'll know it's not Grant who's rejecting him. He'll know it's his stepmum – it's always been his stepmum. And as there's no love lost there, that's not going to rock his world in itself, is it?'

I agreed that, no, it wouldn't. And thanked John for at least calling them and trying. But, boy, was I in for a surprise.

And that very afternoon, as well. It was just after three thirty when he rounded the corner, and his body language was already ringing warning bells. I'd been on pins a little, wondering what might or might not have transpired in school, and, in readiness – though I wasn't sure how much help it would be, really – had prepared his favourite tea of pizza and fries, followed by apple pie and custard, which we'd eat together, just the two of us. Mike was going round to Kieron's straight after school to do some fiddling with some recording equipment with him, so we would have the house to ourselves.

Seeing him now made my face fall – clearly something had happened – but I plastered a smile on as he came through the front door. 'Hi, love,' I said. 'How's you? How was school today?'

'Humph!' he said, as he peeled off his bag. His coat was already in a twizzle round the shoulder strap, and I took both from him, separating them as he yanked down the hem of his school shirt and placed his angry fists once again on his hips. 'Humph!' he huffed again.

I went into the kitchen, and he followed.

'Go on,' I said, 'spit it out.'

'Casey,' he said, 'you will *never* guess what. Our Grant. He can go do one as far as I'm concerned. I have totally, *totally* had it with him.'

'What happened, love?' I asked, fearing the worst.

'I never had a chance to give him the invitation, even!' he thundered. 'He just came straight up to me at first break and started having this big go at me! Said I'd really upset Mum – *his* mum, I told him that *right* off. Said she was fed up with me telling lies about her – me! – an' that Dad was fuming. Said I was bringing so much shit down on their

131

heads and that I was to stop being a twat or he wouldn't speak to me any more. And *he* was the one who said "twat", Casey. Not me.' He paused only to take in air. 'Can you *believe* that?'

'No, love, I can't,' I said, even though as soon as he'd said it I really could. Of course this would happen – I should have realised. Divide and rule, wasn't it? But this was not the place to be fanning fires or increasing acrimony. 'But something must have happened, mustn't it? For Grant to say things like that to you. He's your little brother. He loves you. He –'

'I know what's happened,' Tyler barked, looking worryingly like he might soon reprise his raging bull persona. 'I know exactly what's happened. It's John and Will going round, isn't it? She'll have gone mad, wouldn't she? Started lying about me again, like she always does – and she'll have done it. She'll have told him loads of bad shit about me and told him I gotta fuck off out their lives. That's what's happened!'

'Oh, love,' I began.

'Yeah, an' that's fine by me,' he spat. 'Cos you know what? I never, not *ever*, thought Grant would believe it. He's even seen some of the shitty things she's done to me – he knows!' He paused to inhale again, two pink spots flaming on his cheeks now. 'So I never gave it him. I told him I'd like to stick his party invitation where the sun doesn't shine. I gave it to Danny Ellis in year 9 instead – and I wasn't even planning on inviting him, cos he's only Cam's friend really, but I was that mad I did! Honest, Casey – I really was. I was that *mad*!'

I nodded my understanding, but didn't go to put my arms around him. He was angry rather than tearful and I felt he'd probably shake me off, and a part of me felt glad that Grant had roused his anger rather than made him cry – in some way, it made the rejection feel less like a rejection – as the power (the power of the pool party invite, now withdrawn) had been firmly in Tyler's hands. I was also gladdened by the level of his emotional intelligence. Despite his fury, he had understood that Grant's treatment of him had a very defined root, in the shape of Alicia and the seeds she'd planted in her brother's mind. All of which was good, and would help him on the journey he had to make. But, damn them, it was rejection, all the same.

'Oh, sweetie,' I said, 'that's not very nice, is it? But, hey, you have your friends coming and you'll have a great party, and it's his loss. But you know,' I said, risking placing a hand on his shoulder, 'your Grant's like piggy in the middle a bit here, isn't he? I'll bet your parents – I mean, Alicia and your dad – have been giving him a bit of a hard time, and he's stuck not knowing which way to turn. He's bound to feel he has to be loyal to them, but he also wants to be a good brother … it can't be easy for him, all this, can it?'

'They're *not* my parents.'

'I know … I'm sorry, love.'

'She never was anyway and he's not no more, either. I'm not bothered no more anyway. Forget 'em. Forget them *all*. And you can tell them – whatever they send round for me on Thursday, I don't want it, okay? They can stick their birthday presents up their arses!'

And with that decisive comment – grimly echoing what his father had said only a few days previously – Tyler rolled up his shirtsleeves and yanked out a kitchen chair. 'Right,' he said, 'I'm starving. What's for tea?'

Chapter 12

Tyler cried later, just as I'd known he would. We had our tea, during which all he talked about was the coming party, and then, when Mike came home, he recounted the whole thing again to him. Which was a good sign, I thought, in the midst of such a bleak situation – at least it indicated how close he now felt to us. I was also gratified to watch how intently he listened to Mike when he said much the same as I had about Grant's difficult situation, and how readily he seemed to take all that on board.

We then watched the usual soaps, and he did his usual flurry of texting – no doubt filling in interested parties about the injustices that had been done to him. And that was fine. I knew he needed to get it off his chest.

It was only when we went to bed ourselves that I became aware of the almost inaudible sound of crying; he was clearly doing his best to try and be sure we didn't hear.

I went and knocked on his door softly. It was ajar anyway, so I also pushed it open, and he immediately turned towards me, scrubbing at his face.

'You okay, love?' I whispered. 'Shall I come in for a bit? You want a cuddle?' Without waiting for an answer, I padded across to the bed.

He wriggled up and had his face buried in my chest almost as soon as I sat down, and I held him tight, letting the sobs come, rubbing his back.

'I know,' I said softly. 'I know how much it hurts, love.'

To which his answer was to simply hold me tighter.

We must have sat there like that for a good 20 minutes. He didn't seem to want to talk, and I didn't try to make him. Then, finally, he pulled away and sniffed. His eyes were puffy, his ridiculously long lashes clumped together, as he looked at me. 'I'm sorry,' he whispered.

'Sweetheart, why on *earth* would you be sorry?' I whispered back. 'We all need to cry sometimes. That's what makes us human. And, listen you, that's what I'm *here* for.'

He gave me a wan smile and asked me if he could have a drink of water. So I went downstairs and got him one, my heart filling up every bit as much as the glass I was holding. *God*, what I wouldn't like to say to certain persons, and in no uncertain terms.

I padded back upstairs, into Tyler's bedroom, and placed the glass on his bedside cabinet. Then tiptoed out again. He was already fast asleep.

In the end, we bought Tyler a new mobile phone. Levi had soon forgotten about his secret mission to find our what Tyler wanted for his birthday, but one thing that had happened during the course of the previous Sunday was that Jackson had come into the kitchen while Kieron and I were washing up asking, 'Nanna, what's a shittyshittyphone?'

Which naturally had both me and Kieron stifling giggles, but also planted the seed of an idea in my head. Even if it wasn't quite as shittyshitty as he obviously deemed it to be – it worked, didn't it? – it was pretty elderly. It was probably even more prehistoric than mine was, which was saying something – and Kieron agreed that any sane boy of his age who didn't already have one would want a smartphone more than pretty much anything.

So off I went to the shops, mostly baffled (as I still am) about smartphone technology, but with a name on a piece of paper provided by my son, and the aim of finding Tyler something called a blackberry.

Or, more correctly, 'BlackBerry', as was written on the note. And I duly got one. To me, it was simply an expensive phone with tiny keyboard buttons – I could barely even see them, let alone use them – but to all the kids (at that time, anyway) they were life support systems. You could go online, access social media, take and store photos, and even watch movies on them apparently. Which was impressive, if slightly baffling, and I was pleased I'd succumbed, even though it cost way more than we'd intended spending.

I got it home, wrapped it and added it to the little pile – one that already included gifts from Riley and David, Kieron and Lauren and, bless them, my mum and dad, who'd grown very fond of our latest addition to the family.

There was only one notable absence – anything from Tyler's own family, a circumstance that had been on my mind since he'd made his pithy comment about what they could do with their gifts. Would there even *be* anything for him?

I knew that, subconsciously, it had been that possibility that had been instrumental in my and Mike's impulsive decision to buy him such an expensive gift. Not that money could buy happiness – any idiot already knew that – any more than could the lavish birthday breakfast I had prepared for him fill the hole in the present pile.

He was thrilled to bits when I told him what we were having, even so. 'Pancakes, with strawberries, cream *and* syrup for the birthday boy,' I announced when he came down. 'Go on, go and sit at the table and open up your presents, then we'll get stuck into them, okay?'

Tyler looked in wonderment at the pile of gaily wrapped gifts. 'These are *all* for me? From you?' he asked, looking genuinely staggered by this news.

'Not all from me and Mike – there's gifts from all the family,' I told him. 'Go on, get stuck into them. It might be your birthday but you still have to be at school on time, love.'

He needed no further prompting, opening the one from my parents first, which was a pair of new football socks and a DVD. 'Look, Casey,' he said excitedly, 'it's a goals one! That's epic!'

Equally epic was the present from Kieron and Lauren, which was a book. 'It's the Rooney book!' he said, doing a fist pump. 'Yesss! And look – it's even brand new!'

It made me smile to see his joy at being given a brand new book (was that a first?) even though I wasn't really sure what Rooney had done to elicit such excitement, bar being some footballer or other. But excited Tyler was, eagerly diving in to check out the photos in it.

'Come on,' I chivvied. 'Next one!'

He duly obliged, opening a series of boxes to reveal a crisp 20 pound note – his artfully wrapped gift from Riley and David. 'Whoah! A full 20, all for me!' he gasped. He looked at me earnestly then. 'Casey, I might just treat you and Mike to a meal with this. Take you for a pizza or some-thing and then maybe open a bank account with the rest. Now I'm 12 I *should* have a bank account, shouldn't I?'

I smiled. 'That's very sweet of you, Tyler,' I said. 'But no need to buy us a pizza. That money is for you to spend on *you*, love. Or save – and yes, of course we can set you up with a bank account. And then we'll treat *you* to a pizza to celebrate.'

But by now he wasn't even listening, as he'd opened the final package – the one I'd put at the bottom of the pile specially.

'Oh my God, oh my God, oh my *God*! A BlackBerry! Oh, Casey, thanks soooooo much! I've always wanted one of these! Oh God, this is epic – can I take it to school? Will you and Mike set it up for me? Has it got credit?'

'No, yes and yes,' I laughed. 'Calm down, kiddo! No, you can't take it to school – you know they're not allowed, and yes, Mike will do that and yes, we've put on some credit. Now. Pancakes. How many d'you think you can eat?'

'At least four,' he said with some conviction, as I duly dished them up for him. 'Oh, this is my best birthday ever!' He munched happily for a bit on his sticky, gooey mess, then something crossed his face and I knew what might be coming. 'Did anything come from my dad yet?' he asked once he'd swallowed his latest mouthful.

'No, love,' I said quickly, keeping my tone light. 'The postman doesn't get here till you've gone to school, does he? Speaking of which, look at the time – chop chop, now! We've both got a busy day ahead, what with your party and everything, haven't we?'

And though his mouth was too full of pancake again for him to answer, the shadow of anxiety on his face had gone away. I just hoped there'd be no cause for it to return.

Arriving almost on cue, just after Tyler had headed off to school, the postman, predictably, had nothing. And I cursed myself for allowing either of us to even hope he might. But a part of me hoped anyway. They were his parents, for God's sake! Well, his parent and legal guardian, which amounted to the same thing in my book. And how could anyone be so cruel as to punish a kid like that? No, they would surely have something for him – perhaps via John or Will even?

I was clutching at straws and I knew it. And as the little voice in my head kept reminding me, there were lots and lots of parents who'd be cruel enough to punish a kid like that. Who was I kidding?

I called Will. Perhaps he knew something I didn't, either way, and though I knew he'd spoken to his brother about having the inflatable for the party, he might well have forgotten that today was the actual day. Which, of course, he wouldn't have, I realised, even as I heard the ring tone. He was coming to the flipping party, wasn't he?

'They've said nothing to me, Casey,' he said, also predictably. 'Sorry. I did nudge them, though. Told them they could have your address if they needed it and everything. D'you want me to give them a call and find out? Can't hurt.'

Well, it could – they could tell him to take a running jump, couldn't they? And after the previous week's débâcle they might well. But this wasn't about fighting social services – this was about remembering a child's birthday. And if they'd not got anything perhaps they'd at least be guilted into doing so. Yes, it would be late, but I could make something up about that if need be …

I was still pondering that when the phone rang again, and I crossed my fingers as I picked it up. And it was Will again – the unhappy bearer of bad news.

'There's not going to be a present,' he said flatly. 'Beyond belief, all this is. It was him – Gareth – and he seemed shocked I was even asking. Not this year, he said. All about learning lessons. Said Tyler had crossed a line and needed to learn "what was what" – to use his parlance. That it wouldn't be right to reward him with a present after what he did.'

'*What?*' the word exploded out of me. 'But it's his bloody *birthday*! And how the hell can they expect him to follow that sort of twisted logic? He did wrong. They took him to bloody court for that, for God's sake. And he's *been* punished! Jesus! What the hell am I supposed to say to the poor kid?'

'God knows,' said Will, 'but whatever it is, I suggest you count to ten before you say it. I'm so sorry. I tried my best

– even offered to drive over and pick up a card at least, but the phrase "didn't want to know" doesn't even cover it.'

'It's really true, isn't it?' I said dejectedly. 'They really do want him out of their lives, don't they? This whole thing – this whole going to court thing – has all been part of the plan, hasn't it? Given it to them on a plate – a reason to get shot of him. God, I feel like swearing, I really do.'

'I know,' he said. 'And I don't know what to say to you. Look, I'll be seeing you later anyway – you want me to take him to one side, have a chat, you know, once the party's done?'

'*I* know what to say,' I said. 'To certain people, anyway. Particularly to that Alicia – she's behind all of this, I know it. But I won't. I'll hold my tongue for Tyler's sake. And thanks, Will – that's kind of you, but it's okay. I'll handle it.'

Not that I had the faintest idea how.

In the end I decided it would be better to let Tyler enjoy his party before dropping the bombshell that his so-called family had so badly let him down. I whizzed him upstairs as soon as he got in from school with instructions to get changed as quickly as he could so that we could be at the leisure centre before any of his friends arrived.

And he didn't even ask me, which made me feel sure he'd been thinking – that it had been on his mind all that day, same as mine. And that (perhaps as a consequence of seeing Grant? I didn't know) he'd decided to block it out, let well alone. And, sad as it was, that was another example of his emotional intelligence; he was protecting himself, shutting it out – I'd have put money on it.

It was also a blessing because it let me off the hook – for at least the next couple of hours, I wouldn't have to break his heart again.

And the party was a roaring success. While Riley and I sat poolside and watched, Tyler and his pals (and Will, bless him) had the best time in the water; even the skinny 15-year-old who'd come alone on the bus and who had so shyly introduced himself as Cameron.

'Is that the lad he's always hung out with?' Riley wanted to know.

I nodded. 'Another horribly neglected kid, by all accounts.'

'Hmm …' Riley said. 'Either that, or he's taking some-thing he shouldn't be, I reckon.'

I nodded grimly. 'From what Tyler's mentioned, I think it's a bit of both, love.'

There was no mention of Grant's absence by anyone, though, and I was very thankful. It only reared its head at the end when the mums began arriving, and though it might just have been me reading something into nothing I could almost see Tyler's mind working. Why not me? I could sense him thinking. Why can't I have a normal family like everyone else?

Why indeed?

There was still the small – huge – matter of his presents to address, and as we headed home, having dropped the enig-matic Cameron at a designated corner on the way, I could feel the weight of having to tell Tyler what I'd been told pressing down on me.

There was a short reprieve, in that Mike had set up the BlackBerry for him, but I knew it was only a matter of minutes before he *would* ask the question – either that or he resolutely wouldn't ask the question, which would be worse, because then it would just sit there.

'So nothing came, then,' he said, as I put his swimming things in the washing machine. It wasn't a question.

I shook my head. 'It doesn't matter,' he added quickly. 'I knew they wouldn't send nothing. Why would they send me a present after what they said to Grant?'

I tried to keep him positive. It was almost a knee-jerk reaction. 'I know what you're saying, love,' I reassured him. 'But that doesn't mean they won't. I mean, I know things are difficult right now and that your dad might be a bit cross with you, but, but you know, that might change once Alicia calms down about it all, mightn't it? And then it'll be like two birthdays, won't it?'

I could have kicked myself even as the words were coming out of my mouth. Why was I saying that when all my instincts – and the current facts – told me it wasn't true?

Tyler had no truck with it either. 'She won't calm down. She hates me. And my dad don't love me neither. It's okay,' he said again, but now I could see that his chin was wobbling. I went across and hugged him tight, not caring that it would bring on the tears he was trying so hard not to shed.

They were springing in my own eyes as well, as I held him. 'They just don't love me, Casey,' he sobbed. 'Nobody does!'

'Don't be daft, love,' I said. 'Who couldn't love you? You're a very special boy – and I, for one, am proud of you. And so's Mike. What with everything you've been through, and how well you've managed to handle it …'

But he was shaking his head. 'You're wrong,' he said. 'I'm not special. I'm rubbish. If I was special, why did my mum leave me? Why'd she kill herself like that? I just want a mum, Casey. Just want a mum of my *own*. Just want some-one proper to take *care* of me!'

He pulled away then and looked up at me, his face wet and shiny. 'That's all I want. An' I'll be good, honest. Can't *you* be my mum?'

Chapter 13

It all seemed to fall apart very quickly. As I suppose I should have expected, given how long we'd been fostering now, and given Tyler's heartfelt request for me to become his mum now. How did you *deal* with that? I wished I knew, but it never got any easier, *ever*. In a parallel universe, perhaps all the foster parents in the world could become parents to all the kids who needed parents, but in the real world that simply wasn't the way things worked out. There were just too many kids desperately in need of them.

Yes, it was a course of action some took; there were lots of foster parents who ended up adopting a child they had taken on and, who knew? One day that might happen to us. But right now it wasn't an option. I spent that entire night going over and over everything in my mind, trying to think of a way to explain that Mike and I couldn't become Tyler's parents – but there was no way of ever sugaring such a pill.

I thought back to Justin, the first child we'd ever fostered, right after training, and the number of times we'd chewed over the scenario of keeping him till he'd grown up – of giving up the fostering, almost as soon as we'd begun it, in order to perhaps enable this one child to have a 'normal' life. But that word 'perhaps' was so incredibly loaded; we knew all about that from doing our training. We were there to take on 'difficult' kids, and Justin was very much that – a child who had been so profoundly emotionally damaged that it would never be more than a possibility that he'd be okay, and the same applied to pretty much every child we'd had since.

Yes, some were doing okay so far, but others were struggling and always would – and the reality was that the effects of trauma and abuse in early life often didn't become fully apparent till the child was well into adulthood. That was the deal. That was the kind of fostering we did – tackling the kids who'd been so battered by life and toxic relationships that it was odds-on that they were mentally scarred for life.

And we'd made a pact, Mike and I, about what we were in it for. We had our own cherished kids and grandkids and we needed to consider their needs as well; was it fair to them for us to take on a child who might become a challenging adult? Whose troubles might impact negatively on the whole family for years to come?

It wasn't just that, either – we also had a plan. To help not just one but a series of children – as far as we could anyway – till we got too old and cronky to cope. Perhaps then we'd bow out. Slow down. Concentrate on the currently growing band of grandkids. Who knew? But right now, our decision to keep accepting new kids had, we felt sure, been the right one. We'd had several more since Justin had left us, none of whom we would have been able to take in had we let our hearts hold sway and changed our minds.

Every foster parent will be familiar with the way your thoughts go round and round in such a situation, with the guilt and the indecision and most of all the heartache – in knowing you're going to have to spell all that out to a distressed child. I knew it was *never* going to get any easier, and it wasn't.

In the days that followed, and as the days turned to weeks, and September became October, I watched Tyler slide into an emotional malaise that neither Mike nor I knew how to pull him out from.

It wasn't overt. There were no violent outbursts, and no major tantrums, just a gradual bedding-in of the truth he'd always feared: that he was unloved by his family, that even his little brother had turned against him, and that life was basically as shitty as his old phone.

We tried hard to keep him positive, as did Will, as did the fusty Mr Smart, who'd steadily changed from sermonising about behaviour (or so it seemed when I earwigged from the kitchen) to trying desperately to coax a shred of positivity about the future from his young charge.

I kept dragging him round to Mum and Dad's too – it was one thing that always seemed to brighten him up slightly. As if his relationship with these two jolly elderly people was an oasis of peace and calm amid the mental turmoil of his young life.

But it was his friend Cameron – the boy I'd only briefly met and didn't really know – who seemed to be the main rock to which he clung. Unsurprisingly, really, given that they'd known one another for so long; he was the nearest thing to a loyal older brother he'd ever had.

But Cameron was a troubled lad himself. So it shouldn't have come as any surprise that this was a friendship that wasn't necessarily going to be a good thing. Not given Cameron's age, not given his mildly feral situation, and definitely not given the distinctly dodgy, druggy friends that I knew he mostly hung around with.

Which was a huge worry, because the one thing Mike and I had to do, above all, was to keep Tyler on the straight and narrow and away from anything dodgy, not just because of his supervision order, important though that was. It was also because if he was to have a fighting chance of being placed in a permanent foster home, he had to come across as a kid that someone wouldn't be frightened to take on.

It was a Thursday evening when it all began unravelling. Tyler had been generally good about coming straight home from school if he didn't have any after-school activities – presumably because he was hungry, and because he didn't really have much else to do, particularly if Cameron wasn't around. But today he didn't return, and when it got to five I began getting antsy – particularly when I went up to his bedroom and discovered that the one thing I *couldn't* discover was his BlackBerry. Which meant that he'd taken it to school.

Which was against the rules, and he knew it.

'I have a bad feeling about this,' I said to Mike when he got in from work. 'I just feel it in my bones.'

'Try not to panic, love,' he soothed. 'Perhaps he's just testing the boundaries. You know what kids are like – and I mean *all* kids. Not just kids dealing with the crap Tyler's had to. He's probably gone off to someone's house and it's a serious case of peer pressure stopping him from letting you know. Let's eat our tea and put his under some cling-film for later – I think that's best. Let's not panic till we have to, eh?'

But by eight we had no choice *but* to panic. Without Tyler's phone we had no way of getting hold of any of his friends – his old one was in his bedroom but his sim card was obviously not – and I cursed myself for not having thought about trying to get a couple of their numbers. I was also beginning to wonder quite what we should do, because there was the small matter of the supervision order to take into account. If we alerted anyone in authority – Will, say, or John, or the emergency duty team – we would straight away land Tyler in all sorts of grief, something I made a point of pointing out in my latest voicemail.

But, at the same time, he was just 12 and it would have been both unprofessional and irresponsible not to take one of those steps, and very soon, too. We were fortunate, though – Kieron came to the rescue.

Well, came up with a plan at least, bless him, for which I was very grateful. He'd only popped round to give Mike back his drill – he and Lauren had been putting shelves up – and was supposed to be heading straight home to dinner.

'But why don't we just head out and look for him?' he suggested, once I'd outlined our worries.

'I suppose,' I began. 'But I wouldn't know where to look …'

'I would, Mum,' Kieron answered, 'because I do.'

And I noticed something straight away – that his expression was telling me something he hadn't yet said. Kieron was not good at artifice.

'I suppose you do,' I said, though not loading the statement with any undercurrent. Not yet. Of course he'd know where to look – he was a youth worker, wasn't he? It was his job to know where the kids locally hung out. He and Lauren also volunteered once a week for a local homeless charity, so he also knew where all the druggy and disaffected kids went. There was more to this – I just knew it. And I was right.

'Mum, don't go off on one, okay?'

'About what?' I chipped in.

'About what I'm going to tell you, okay? Mum, I've seen Cameron hanging about. He's down the town centre all the time, smoking dope. And – um – well … I've seen Tyler with him there once as well. I said not to go *off on one*!' he added, presumably seeing my horrified expression. 'It was only once, and it was the daytime and he seemed fine – even said hello to me. And I told him then that it wasn't the place for him to be chilling and sort of implied that if I saw him there again I'd have to tell you too.'

'Great,' I said. '*Great*!' I repeated to Mike, who'd just joined us. He'd gone to get our coats and his car keys, and had only heard the tail end of it.

'So that's what I'm doing *now*,' Kieron pointed out. 'Okay? So shall we go?'

In the end just Kieron and I went, as it made no sense to leave the house empty – Tyler might show up there, after all. So, leaving Mike to hold the fort, we drove down to the town centre, following Kieron's directions, fetching up at what used to be the old central bus station. A disused, concrete area, surrounded by an overgrown patch of wood-land, it was a natural magnet for bored teenagers and those with mischief on their minds, as it was away from the main streets now and not overlooked.

It had little else to commend it as a place for kids to gather and I wondered, as I always did, just where kids of that age were *supposed* to gather – something they were naturally drawn to do – particularly those who didn't have welcoming homes to invite their friends into. It was a bleak part of the town, badly in need of regeneration, and with a bank of smelly, much graffiti-ed shelters at the back. It was grim, and put me in mind of a post-apocalyptic movie.

'This is just so sad,' I whispered as we climbed out of the car and made our way across to where we'd seen the glow of a small bonfire and the young people silhouetted by it. Close up they all looked so horrifyingly young.

'Oh, this is nothing, Mum,' Kieron said. 'There's a couple of places much worse than this – proper hardcore. But that tends to be more the old alkies and so on. This is mainly school kids.'

Yes, I thought sadly, school kids who were often absent from school, puffing on skunk, necking cheap vodka and sniffing aerosols. I'd seen a few of them in my time, for sure. And seen the effects, as well, more to the point. Not to mention having read such frightening things about strong weed, and the potentially catastrophic effects it could have on young minds; science that was only now becoming apparent.

Would Tyler be here? I both hoped he was, because I wanted to find him, and at the same time hoped he wasn't. He was only 12, and I couldn't help but cling to the idea that he might just be round Cameron's playing some shoot-'em-up on an Xbox, so engrossed that he was unaware of the time.

I was disabused of that notion in moments. Kieron was a few steps ahead of me as we crossed the scrubby ground and I guessed there was no major dispersal going on because they both recognised Kieron, who I knew cultivated relationships with these kids, and, with me being five foot nothing, probably assumed I was just another teen.

'Yo, Jamie,' he called out. 'How's it going?'

It was only as we got close that I could see anxious faces beginning to scrutinise me properly, and for a moment I wondered if they'd all go haring off, just like me and my mates used to do when we were 13 or 14 and would be smoking the proverbial fags behind the park pavilion.

How things had changed, I thought. Such innocent times.

'K,' the nearest lad said, which would in other circumstances have tickled me – was that what they knew him as? But not these.

They clasped hands, and even as they did so I could sense a couple of the younger kids melting into the shadows, and it was when one moved that I realised I was looking straight at Cameron – well, someone I thought I recognised as Cameron anyway; it was difficult to be sure in the dark. One thing that I could see, however, was that he hadn't really noticed me. He was sitting off at the side, his back against the one remaining piece of glass at the back of the furthest shelter and, surprisingly, seemed oblivious to our arrival.

Kieron was chatting to the boy called Jamie, explaining that we'd mislaid Tyler, couching it in terms that made it sound a million miles from 'who-is-under-a-supervision-order-and-this-is-serious' kind of talk. I was very impressed. One hint of authority and it would have probably meant a total shut-down. There was a code, I knew, and it was part of their lore that it wasn't broken. It would have been 'No, I ain't seen no one' all round.

But it soon became academic anyway. I touched Kieron's arm. 'That boy over there? The one sitting under that far shelter in the red hoodie? I'm sure that's Cameron. Shall I go and speak to him? See if he knows where Tyler might be?'

I felt a new hope flare. That with Cameron being here and there being no sign of Tyler, perhaps they'd been together earlier and had since parted company. Perhaps Tyler was already back home.

'Let's go and see, shall we?' Kieron said, nodding, and it took us no more than half a dozen strides to be in a position to see that just beyond Cameron was another lad, also sitting with his back against the glass, and who I'd not previously spotted in the gloom. He had one earbud in his ear and I realised he was sharing an iPod with a girl who was sitting on the other side of him. He was obviously listening to music, because though his eyes were half shut his head was nodding rhythmically, along with the girl's.

I felt relief wrapped in gloom. It was Tyler.

He looked stoned. And, perhaps because of that, he was perfectly happy to see us. There was certainly no kind of scene or resistance. 'You coming home, love?' I asked him, and after blinking at me a couple of times he took out the earbud, handing it to the girl who was attached to the other end of it, and got unsteadily to his feet. 'Sure,' he said, brushing ineffectually at the dust on his trousers.

And at that point I was glad no one else was involved because he was silly and giggly, his pupils like black moons in his already dark eyes. A proper little stoner.

'Where's your phone, Ty?' Kieron remembered to ask him as we flanked him and herded him back to my car.

Tyler patted his trouser pocket – it felt so incongruous that he was still in school uniform – then pulled it out with a dreamy smile. 'Always safe!' he slurred.

'Well, at least that's *one* bit of good news,' Kieron said.

Yes, I thought miserably. But only one.

And the day wasn't done with being unkind to us yet. We were home 20 minutes later and I hurried Kieron back out, so he wouldn't be too late for tea. I knew Lauren would understand but I still felt guilty to have landed all that on them both when they'd both had full days at work already.

Mike and I then put Tyler to bed. There was no point in even trying to talk to him, much less remonstrate with or lecture him. That would have to wait till he was sober and free of the effects of whatever he'd taken, something we didn't as yet even know.

'I suppose I could have asked Cameron,' I said to Mike, once we were back downstairs clutching mugs of coffee, 'but at the time it seemed the best thing was just to get him and *go*.'

'I would have done the same, love, don't worry,' Mike said. 'And would you have found out anyway? If they're all stoned, would anyone have anything sensible to tell you? No, you did the right thing. And the best thing is for him to sleep it off now.' He laughed mirthlessly. 'Are you on first watch or am I?'

I laughed too – also without humour: what a night we had in store. I'd been around enough to know he was probably not in imminent danger, but you never knew. And, in any event, he might be sick. No, vigilance was all in these kinds of situations, which I thought was what must have been the cause of Mike's heavy sigh. But apparently not. 'Case,' he said, 'there's something else.'

'Something else?' I said, conscious of his serious expression. 'What sort of something else? End of the world something else?'

'Not quite,' he said. Then he shook his head. 'No, not at all. It's to do with your mum and dad –'

'Oh, God,' I said, frightened now. 'What? Is Dad okay?'

He was quick to reassure me. 'No, no, love – I just told you – *not* the end of the world. He's absolutely fine. No, it's about Tyler again.'

I was confused now. 'In what way?'

'Well, you know after you and Kieron left? Well, I had this brainwave. It was only an outside chance, admittedly, but it occurred to me that he might have gone round there. Silly, I know –'

'That's not silly.'

'Well, it is a bit – they would have called you, wouldn't they?'

'Not necessarily. Not if they thought I already knew he was round there. Which he wasn't, of course, but – sorry. Go on.'

'Well, I was telling them what had happened – how you and Kieron had gone out to look for him, and, you know – just saying that we were worried about him, how things have been since his birthday and so on, and your mum told me ...'

He paused.

'*What*?'

'That your dad had seen him take a tenner out of your mum's purse when he was round there last week, basically. She said they didn't want to believe it, but they had no choice, apparently. Your dad was watering the window box under the kitchen window, and saw him doing it with his own eyes.'

He drained his coffee cup and stood up – headed to the kettle again, no doubt. It was going to be a long night, after all, bless him.

'Did Tyler see him?'

'Apparently not,' Mike said. 'And your dad decided not to say anything till he spoke to your mum. They were going to tell us about it at the weekend. Bless them – they felt awful about it, and really didn't want to get him into more trouble …'

'I think we're past that point now, don't you?' I said, handing him my empty mug.

Great, I thought. Brilliant. I put a hand on Mike's arm. 'Don't worry, love,' I said. 'You get off to bed. You've got work, haven't you?' I smiled again, grimly. What else could you do?

'I'll do first watch *and* second watch,' I told him. I doubted I'd be sleeping a wink after all.

Chapter 14

I hardly knew where to start. After a night during which I probably wore out a whole swathe of landing carpet with my to-ing and fro-ing, I fell into a deep sleep at around 6 a.m., only to be rudely awakened half an hour later by Mike having his shower.

I dragged myself up to a sitting position and fell gratefully upon the mug of coffee he'd left for me, the events of the previous evening clamouring for attention in my head. Where did I start? Who did I talk to first? What should be the plan?

With consciousness, however, came calm and clarity. I needed to speak to Tyler to get some more facts, finish writing the log that I'd begun the previous evening, then email it to John, and copy it to Will. I'd also hit upon another potentially helpful plan in the wee hours, but I needed to run it by Mike before discussing it – ideally before he headed off to work.

'Tyler's okay,' was the first thing he said when he returned from the bathroom. 'Awake, busy texting, contrite – oh – and grey.' He shook his head as he dried himself. 'Things we do, eh?' he mused. 'One minute, our lives are all quiet on the western front – well, comparatively – the next we're in the middle of a bloody war zone.'

'Did you get much sleep?' I asked him, feeling guilty about the dark smudges under his eyes, even though I knew I had no reason to. It had been a joint decision to take on Tyler, after all. But, still ...

'Enough,' he said. 'More than you did, love, at any rate. Are we sending him into school? Because you look like you need to schedule a "power nap", or whatever they're called.'

'Thanks a bunch,' I said. But then I nodded my agreement. 'I feel about as powerful as a wet dishcloth right now,' I agreed. 'Plus I have some important conversations to have, don't I? Yes,' I said, 'I think he *should* go to school. Christ, he went to bed at 9 p.m. and slept right through, so he can hardly claim he's too tired, can he? And if he has a hangover, well, it'll be a lesson learned, won't it? One of several we have to start teaching him as a matter of some urgency. *God*,' I said with feeling, yanking the duvet off and swinging my legs round. 'I need a bacon and egg sandwich and I need it *now*.'

I felt much better once I was downstairs with my hands wrapped around another mug of coffee and my lovely husband doing his thing with the frying pan. I'd looked in on Tyler, of course, but had kept it brief and to the point. That we'd talk later, that he was going to school and that he needed to be downstairs for his breakfast in 40 minutes, all of which pronouncements were met with meek, whey-faced acceptance. In truth, I think he *wanted* to go to school – it was probably way preferable to spending the day with me lecturing him – and I was happy that, today, he *would* come straight back home again; that I didn't need to baby him by insisting on picking him up. It was all about trust, and it mattered that he didn't abuse mine. I figured that he knew what the consequences would be.

I had no idea why I felt so confident that Tyler wouldn't abuse our faith in him, but, for some reason, despite the disappearing acts – of both him and that tenner – I did. Lack of sleep-induced mania? Perhaps. In any event, while he got showered and dressed upstairs, I quickly ran my half-plan by Mike, so that I could put it to John when I spoke to him later.

We had a friend called Bob, who was a policeman. We'd known him since our twenties, and though he'd moved away we'd kept in touch. And now, following a divorce, he was back in our area, and I knew he wouldn't mind helping out. 'So I was thinking that perhaps we could get in touch with him,' I suggested to Mike. 'See if he'll maybe do some work with Tyler – you know, educating him about the dangers of drugs; the sort of horrible things they can lead to.'

Mike nodded. 'Well, he's certainly the one to do it,' he agreed. 'I doubt there's much he *hasn't* seen, don't you?'

He was right. Bob had been on the drug squad for years, and, back in the day, would regale us with tales of dealers and addicts and situations that were invariably pretty shocking – tales that underlined that everything in the movie *Trainspotting* was true. But Tyler was an innocent still – well, comparatively – and although he already had good reason to fear drugs (that being how he lost his mother) I knew how easily a young boy could blank all the rational thinking that was required if you were going to keep saying 'no'.

'I think it would be so good for him,' I said. 'I know he might only have been smoking a bit of weed, but, God, he's so *young* still …'

'And weed isn't weed any more, is it?' Mike pointed out. 'Not like the stuff that used to be around. It's potent. And pretty scary. Could do all sorts of damage.'

'Exactly,' I said, 'plus I'm hoping it will reassure John that he can leave us to handle things, rather than bringing in anyone else. Or running it by Mr Smart and probably making everything even worse. I mean, I know it'll all have to go on his file, but I'm sure I can convince John we can handle it.'

'I don't doubt that for a minute,' Mike said, chuckling as he plonked a mouth-watering-looking doorstep in front of me. 'But right now, see how well you can handle that.'

The things we were currently dealing with – a kid smoking dope and stealing a tenner from a family member – were nothing we hadn't dealt with before. And in the big scheme of behaviours we'd had to address as foster carers over the years this was relatively mild.

So once I'd got on the outside of my sandwich and topped up my reserves of positivity I was able to put things in the right kind of perspective, i.e. bad, but not heart-in-mouth bad. And when Tyler came down and I could see the remorse in his manner, I thought that, actually, there was much to be positive about. He knew he'd done wrong – he understood that he had let Mike and me down. It didn't matter so much if he didn't think his high-jinks with dope were that dangerous – I'd recruit Bob to address that particular childish misconception – but it did matter that he understood that he'd let us down personally, and felt bad. And in that I felt we did have a result.

'Are you gonna ring social services and have them take me back now?' was almost the first thing he said, once he'd told me he was sorry and he was absolutely ravenous. Which wasn't surprising, since, though he hadn't been sick at any point, he probably hadn't eaten anything of substance since he'd left school the previous afternoon.

'No, we're not,' I said mildly, while I stirred the porridge he'd requested. 'Because that's not the way me and Mike do things.' I nearly added – instinctively – that 'sending kids back' wasn't an option for parents, was it? And thank God my mouth wasn't too far ahead of my brain, because that's precisely what his own 'parents' had done. 'The way I see it, Tyler, is that we took you in with a plan – a plan to teach you a bit more about life's realities – how to approach it, how to behave, how to treat people …' I glanced across at the fridge-freezer. 'That's what that chart there is for. So you can learn that the best way to live a useful and happy life is to behave well and treat people with respect.'

I put the porridge in front of him, then pulled out another chair and sat down on it. 'Tyler,' I said, 'we're cross you put us through so much nonsense last night, of course we are. Look at the bags under my eyes – I've got to go to Tesco looking like this. But mostly we're worried about *you*. Yes, it's your body and once you're an adult you can choose to fill your body up with stupid drugs, but right now you're a child and we're here to keep you from harm. And now you're almost a teenager, that's not a case of keeping you physically contained, like you were a toddler. It's a case of giving you the wherewithal to control your *own* behaviour; of you learning that if you're hell bent on being irrespon-sible, that's a choice – a choice *you* make – and that there will almost *always* be consequences.'

It was a little speech that would come back to haunt me, but right now I decided it was enough to be going on with. He needed to get to school and to reflect and then we'd talk again later. It was at the forefront of my mind that there was another important matter we still had to talk about – the business of the money he had purloined from my mum, presumably to give him the funds for last night's bit of fun.

'Dear me, there's nothing new under the sun, is there, Casey?' was John's pronouncement once, having waved Tyler off, I'd sent him the email and he'd phoned for the low-down.

'Tell me about it,' I said, stifling my zillionth yawn of the morning. 'I'm obviously going to tackle him about the money once he gets in from school, but I'm confident we can handle it if you are.'

'Oh, absolutely,' he said. 'I have no worries on that score. And to be honest, I'm not surprised things have taken a bit of a slide. Given how blatantly the family have rejected him, it would really have been much more surprising if he *hadn't* kicked off in some way. All that hurt and anger's got to be expressed somehow, hasn't it? And I suppose a bit of light pilfering and drug-dabbling behind the bus shelter – however bad – has got to be better than another episode of violence. Not that I'm condoning it, obviously.'

'No, of course not,' I said. 'But yes, you're right. And his remorse feels genuine, too. Course, that's not to say we won't have some sort of rumpus *re* the money. I just hope he owns up to it, that's all.'

Which he did. Immediately. As soon as I brought it up. He was home dead on time, just as I'd optimistically predicted, and I saw no point in putting off tackling him about it – the sooner it was out there, the sooner it could be dealt with. The only reason I'd not spoken to him about it that morning, really, was because I felt it was too much to risk a double-whammy of tellings-off; whatever I might have said to him, I knew it might just create enough anxiety in his mind that he contemplated a fall-back of running away to escape it.

But we were back in my kitchen – him with a glass of milk, me with a coffee – and I only had to say 'Tyler, I've been talking to my dad …' for tears to gather in his eyes.

Tyler being the age he was, I'd half-expected an immediate denial. So many kids – the kids we dealt with – practised the 'I ain't done nothing' rule. Deny everything, so the logic went, unless the evidence was overwhelming. And then keep at it – just deny it some more. Or if not – some schtick about how he was only borrowing it, or some such. But here we were, with me not even having accused Tyler of anything, and there were already tears tracking down his cheeks. I remained silent for a few moments, while he sat there and squirmed, hands clasped in his lap, gaze directed at the table.

'Tyler,' I said eventually. 'Is there something you need to tell me?'

Yes. There clearly was. And he did. Well, not in detail, since he didn't really need to. He told me he'd nicked the tenner and that he just did it on the spur of the moment, and that as soon as he'd done it he wished he'd hadn't and that he promised he'd pay it back.

I told him I knew. And that I believed him. And that, though he was rather light on points now, I would see that he did. And that the most important thing I had to say to him was the same as I'd said that morning: that it was all about treating people the way you'd want to be treated and that he must *never* do anything like that again.

And he just cried and cried, sitting at the table, head sitting on crossed forearms, and I left him to it, and pottered around the kitchen, knowing that he was crying because he felt bad about what he'd done, which by any yardstick was a very positive thing.

After a few minutes, when he finally raised his head, I was ready, passing him a wodge of kitchen roll so he could wipe his face.

'There,' I said. 'Better?'

He nodded wanly as he blew his nose.

'Come on,' I said, holding a hand out. 'Come here.'

He looked confused at first, anxious, unsure what was expected of him, and I thought angrily of the stepmother who'd knocked him about, and, when not hitting him, had been so cruel and cold.

'What?' Tyler asked, edging round the kitchen table.

I changed the hand to both arms to make things clearer. 'I want a hug,' I said, 'and I think you could use one too, couldn't you?'

He stepped into my arms then and I held him tight, kissing the top of his head, which, of course, made him start crying all over again.

But that was okay, I thought. That was just as it should be.

Chapter 15

My mum and dad didn't want to make a big fuss about everything, but it was important Tyler face them, so I wheeled him round there that weekend and had him say sorry to them both personally, as well as reassure them he'd be paying them back just as soon as he'd earned sufficient pocket money.

I knew my mum would have told him not to worry, so I'd primed her first and they both managed to look sufficiently stern as he mumbled his apologies.

And that was where I thought we'd leave things. But it seemed I was wrong.

'Here, Casey,' Tyler said to me the following Saturday morning, shoving a folded-over piece of paper into my hand. It was torn from an exercise book.

'What's this?' I asked him.

'It's for Grandad,' he said. 'And Nan as well,' he added, blushing furiously.

I was confused for half a second, wondering what he was talking about, as there'd never been mention of any grand-parents being in the picture before.

'Grandad?' I asked.

'Your dad,' he corrected. Then adding 'That's what *he* told me to call him' somewhat defensively. 'He did, *honest*. He said it sounded silly to call him Mr Watson and that he liked Grandad better.' Which made me feel terrible. It would have been just like my dad to do that – as far as he was concerned, why not? And now Tyler felt he had to justify being granted permission to use a term up to now he'd not had the privilege of using for anyone. I could have kicked myself.

'Of course,' I said, nodding. 'I know that, love. I was just wondering what about him. You want me to give this to him then, do you?'

He nodded. 'It's just a letter to say a proper sorry. You know, about that tenner. I feel bad that he thinks I'm a robber now. I mean I know he won't want me doing his roses or anything no more, or anyway, an' it's not asking him to or anything. I just wanted to, like, tell him I'm sorry … You can read it if you like.'

Now I'd gone from wanting to kick myself to needing to dislodge the lump forming in my throat. What a learning curve this whole business was turning out to be.

I smiled at him. 'No, no, it's not for me, is it? So I won't read it. But I'm popping round later, while you're out with your friends, so I'll give it to him then. And, Tyler,' I added, dropping slightly to be at his level, 'thanks *so* much for this, love. Dad'll really appreciate it. It's a very grown-up thing to do and, even better, no one even asked you to do it, so it's extra special, and don't you worry – I'm sure Dad'll still want your help. He says you're an excellent little gardener.'

All of which was true. Though he'd recovered well since his op, he'd still lost a bit of his get up and go, and Tyler had proved to be an unexpected tonic for him. Mum had confided that, more than that, even, he'd really enjoyed having him around because he could have a joke with him and pass on all the many words of manly wisdom that Kieron was too busy and grown-up to listen to often these days and that Levi and Jackson were still a bit small for.

'He's been a blessing,' my mum had said. 'Really helped get your dad back on track.' And, fingers firmly crossed, that meant two of them.

Tyler's cinema trip had been hard won, and that was as it should have been. He couldn't have worked harder to earn enough points to make it happen, and as it was with a couple of mates from school – mates who were his own age – I was particularly keen to see it happen. Though we'd yet to fix up a visit from Bob to chat to him about drugs, we'd been laying the groundwork, gently trying to impress upon Tyler that Cameron and his other older friends weren't necessarily doing stuff that he wanted to be getting into – though still trying to be very softly-softly about it. These were his mates and he obviously felt very loyal.

'Now don't you be getting into any trouble,' I warned as I pulled up outside the cinema complex a couple of hours later to drop him off. He promised he wouldn't. 'And call me as soon as you come out,' I added, 'and either Mike or I will come and fetch you, okay?'

He chewed his lip for a second or two, making no move to get out of the car.

'Okay?' I said again.

'Yeah, yeah,' he said, 'only, Casey, it's just that they're going for a pizza straight after – only next door. Right there.' He pointed. 'And I know I don't have enough points and that, but could I sort of –'

I cut him off, having decided. 'Yes, okay, you can. Just an extra hour, okay? And you make sure you ring us in good time so we can be here before your mates leave. I don't want you hanging about in the dark.'

'Yay!' he said, doing a little fist pump before leaning across to kiss my cheek. 'That's *epic*!'

'Yes, well, don't forget I'll be leaving you some spring cleaning chores to do tomorrow, will you?'

'Casey,' he said, giggling, 'you can't *spring* clean. It's October!'

'Off with you,' I said, shooing him out of the car. 'When it comes to cleaning, I can do anything I flipping like!'

Dad, as I'd expected, was thrilled to get Tyler's note. He read it straight away, his eyes glistening, I noticed, as he took off his reading glasses. 'He's not a bad lad,' he said. 'Given everything, he could be a lot, lot worse, couldn't he?' *And he should know*, I thought, with us having exposed him to so many damaged foster kids now. 'And there's the proof, right there,' he said, waggling the piece of paper, 'that he's got it in him to know when he's done wrong.'

Well, once he'd been found out, anyway, I thought, but didn't say. And, actually, Dad made a good point. He'd obviously been dying to confess, hence those tears before I'd even asked him, and, more to the point, he had already apologised and been told that was the end of the matter. Yet it had obviously still been eating at him, and that was an encouraging sign of empathy. So, after two cups of coffee and a slice of my mum's lemon drizzle cake, I felt a real spring in my step as I headed home to my spring cleaning. Even if it was October.

I got stuck straight in, too, as was always my way. I didn't know what it was about cleaning the house that I loved so much, but I had an inkling that over the years it had probably saved me a fortune in headache pills and therapy. Particularly when I got really into it, pulling out appliances, washing down walls and skirtings, and generally ousting every scrap of grime.

I was so engrossed that I didn't even hear my mobile ringing, and it was Mike who answered Tyler's call to be brought home.

'You go,' he suggested, 'while I clear up your cleaning things. I don't know, Case – I swear this kitchen looks messier than it did when you started!'

'Oh nonsense,' I chided, stripping off my Marigolds. 'It's pristine! Well, it will be once you've pushed the cooker and the fridge-freezer back, and, um, emptied the bucket and squeezed the mop and put all the cleaning stuff away.'

He rolled his eyes and I headed out of the door.

* * *

It was just dark by the time I returned to the cinema complex and it was a few moments before I could make Tyler out, standing with a couple of other lads by the far corner of the building.

I wasn't sure I recognised them – were they the lads who he'd run to when I'd dropped him off? I peered closer to the windscreen to try and get a better look. No, they weren't. They were definitely a lot bigger than Tyler, and as I drew up in the car I could see that one of them was smoking a cigarette – or something more sinister.

But they were certainly friends; I could tell that by the way they were all joshing with each other and laughing. I switched off the engine and opened the car door.

Tyler saw me then, and, after waving a farewell to the other boys, jogged over the tarmac to the car.

'Who are they?' I asked him as we climbed back in. 'They're not the boys you went with, are they?'

He shook his head and reached for his seatbelt. 'No, that's Carl and James. They're mates of Cam's. I just bumped into them – they're going in to the next showing.'

'What happened to your other mates?'

'Oh, they just got picked up by Dan's mum. She said she'd drop me but I told her you were on your way, and I said it was all right because Carl and James were there.'

Which was fair enough, I supposed. 'Tyler,' I had to ask, though, 'was one of them smoking dope? You know how I feel about that, don't you? You know, boys of that age ...'

I was already wishing I hadn't said it even as I did, and maybe I was right to. 'No!' he said, genuinely indignant. 'It was just a proper fag! God's sake! Can't I even talk to them now? They're my friends!'

They were still standing there, watching us leave, and I felt bad. They were just lads themselves. Older lads, yes, and, yes, they probably did smoke dope, but that didn't mean they weren't loyal, longstanding mates. And it wasn't for me to judge – no, my own kids wouldn't have hung around with much older lads, but that was due to circumstance – Tyler's childhood had been very, very different. 'I'm sorry, love,' I said. 'I was just over-reacting, I suppose. I just worry about you, that's all. I just don't want you to get into any trouble.' I smiled, 'Not if it means Mr Smart coming round the house once a week for ever more!'

He lightened up then. 'I know,' he said. 'But you mustn't think everyone's gonna get me into trouble. I *can* think for myself. You *can* trust me.'

Wise words under normal circumstances, but so far life with Tyler had been a long way from that. I ruffled his head and then turned the car around and we set off for home. 'Okay, deal,' I said, 'and if we're lucky, Mike will have finished clearing up the clearing up so we can settle down to telly right away.'

Which was pretty much what we did, punctuated by intense philosophical conversations between Tyler and Mike about both the incredible special effects in the latest *X Men* movie and which superpowers would be the best ones to have. It was a lovely evening – nothing exciting, just relaxing family time in front of the telly – but those were sometimes the best. The ones that made the world go round.

* * *

And if I could have bottled it, maybe I should have.

It was still fully dark when something woke me up. But I'd been asleep a fair while, I could tell. I was very alert, coming fully awake in a matter of moments, blinking as my eyes adjusted to the blackness. I wasn't sure what had disturbed me, but then, a second later, I tuned back into it. A faint rhythmic thudding sound, accompanied by what? Crying? Careful not to disturb Mike, I twisted my legs round and down, out of the bed, and checked the time. A little after four.

Puzzled, I tiptoed out of our bedroom and padded across the landing, realising that I had been right in my guess – it had been the sound of crying, but that strange rhythmic sound, what was that?

Tyler's door was ajar – wide enough for a thread of light to be visible underneath it, and as I pushed it open fully I was faced with the answer to my unspoken question; he was sitting on his bed, mobile phone in hand, crying his eyes out and repeatedly hitting the back of his head against the wall.

'Tyler! What the hell?' I said, rushing across to him, to try and stop him whacking his head. Close up both the sound and the sight were sickening. I managed to swap the hard wall for the softness of my supporting hand, but at the cost of the pain he was inflicting on my knuckles as he continued to thrust his head backwards.

'Tyler!' I snapped, trying to get his attention, 'stop doing that! Stop it! What's wrong? Tyler, you're hurting yourself!'

Had already hurt himself, I realised, feeling the stickiness beneath my fingers and pulling them away to find them smeared with glistening bright red blood, and belatedly realising it was coursing down his neck and dripping from his chin. *Christ*, I thought, how long had he been doing this?

'Mike!' I yelled. 'Mike! Come here! I need you!' I then continued my attempts to stop Tyler's relentless head-banging, grabbing his shoulders and trying to pulling him closer to me and far enough away from the wall that even if he flung his head back it wouldn't make contact.

'Tyler!' I tried again. 'Speak to me, *please*! What's wrong? What's happened? Why are you doing this?'

Now he did seem to notice me, suddenly making eye contact. 'Fuck off, Casey,' he roared, trying to wriggle free. 'He's dead! He's fucking *dead*!'

He pulled free again then and whacked his head back, harder than ever. There was blood smeared all over the wall, I realised. I felt physically sick. Thank God for Mike, then, who swooped in, while I was still trying to wrestle with Tyler, and who, with a 'Move, Casey!', scooped him up as if he was feather-light, clasped him to his chest and carried him out of the room.

I was still trying to take everything in. 'What the hell's happened?' I said as I scrambled up and followed him. 'Who's dead?'

'Never mind that now,' Mike commanded. 'Casey, bathroom light – we need to look at his head.'

I reached for the pull-switch, while Mike grabbed a towel from the rail and pressed it against the back of Tyler's head. The strong male presence had seemingly caused a change in him; he was limp now, thank God, weeping quietly into Mike's chest.

'Okay, lad,' Mike soothed, sitting down carefully on the toilet, with Tyler, who looked so incredibly small in his arms. 'Casey, grab another towel and wet it, please?' he said, carefully moving the one he already had, and I could tell by his intake of breath that it didn't look good.

'Do you think we'll need to go to A&E?' I asked, handing him the fresh one. He nodded. 'Without a doubt. It's a head wound, isn't it? Might not need many stitches,' he added, inspecting it – I didn't really want to look yet – 'but he'll need an X-ray, won't he, given how he's done it.'

Tyler at this time still had his face in Mike's T-shirt, his shoulders moving as rhythmically as his head had been. 'Love, tell us,' I urged him. 'Who's dead? What's happened?' But he just cried all the more and Mike shook his head.

'Love, go and fetch him some trackies and stuff, and get yourself something too. We need to get him down there, and the sooner we go the better.'

'Okay,' I said, hurrying back into the bedroom, and it was while reaching for his clothes that I realised his phone was on the bed.

I picked it up, fully expecting it to be locked, but it wasn't, and scrolling through I could see a couple of indecipherable texts. And a missed call. A missed call that had come in at three thirty, from someone called James.

Not even thinking about it, I pressed call back, and it was answered almost in an instant.

'Ty?' a young male voice said.

'No, this is Casey,' I explained. 'I'm his foster mum. I, er ...' I wasn't sure quite what to say. 'Er, what's happened?'

There was a silence. And I realised that he, too, was crying. 'It's Cam,' he said brokenly. 'He's been killed.'

I didn't say anything for ages. It just all felt too unreal. Not till after we'd arrived at A&E, where we were thankfully seen quickly, not till after Tyler had had his wound stitched, for which they sedated him heavily, not till after he was scanned to check there was nothing else untoward happening, not till after we were allowed to take him home. It was dawn by the time we put him to bed – not in his own bed, but the one in the pink room – though he was so zonked out by drugs, he wouldn't have cared.

'Christ,' Mike whispered, looking at his finally peaceful sleeping face, 'that poor little lad. What he's got to wake up to. So,' he added, as we slipped out and downstairs to the kitchen, 'what did the lad on the phone have to tell you?'

So I told him. That Cameron had been killed in a car crash, in a car he and two friends – not the ones I'd met earlier, other boys, apparently – had stolen while high on some drug. It had hit a lamp-post, and Cameron, who'd been driving and wasn't wearing a seat belt, had died instantly, while the other two had got away with minor injuries.

It was a mess – a bloody mess – and as I recounted it to Mike it made me cry. It was such a senseless, needless loss of a young life. So I cried for Cameron, even though I'd never really known him, and for the tragedy of a life snuffed out because of drugs. But most of all, I cried for the little boy currently sleeping above our heads, who had lost the one thing he had still, the one thing that mattered – Cameron might have been little more than a name to us, but to Tyler he was everything; his much-cherished best and oldest friend.

It didn't matter that his physical injuries had not been deemed to be serious. It was the injury to his emotional well-being that really mattered, and the damage to that had yet to be seen.

Chapter 16

Even though it was a Sunday, I felt I had no choice but to call both John and Will and fill them in on the events of the previous night. Even if I just got their answerphones, it didn't matter – this was important, and given the state Tyler had been in I didn't feel it would be responsible for us to deal with it alone.

I was surprised when John answered his mobile – I'd just been gearing up to recite my message.

'Hi, Casey,' he said cheerfully. 'I'm guessing this isn't a social call? It's not often that your name flashes up on a Sunday.'

'It's not,' I agreed. 'Oh, John. I don't think I even know where to start.'

'That sounds ominous,' he said, his tone changing to match my own. 'How about you just begin at the beginning.'

So I did, and, as I began recounting it, I could feel myself welling up. It came upon me unexpectedly – I'd really no idea it was going to happen, but as soon as the idea of the dead 15-year-old hit my brain again, I just couldn't seem to stop myself crying. It was probably as much a lack of sleep as anything, but when Mike came up behind me, stroking my back and offering to speak to John instead, it was such a struggle to hold myself together that I realised it wasn't just that; it was as much the thought of that little boy upstairs and what we were going to do now. He had no one left – that's what really got to me. Absolutely no one.

Except us. 'It's okay,' I said, to both John and Mike. 'I'll be fine. If you can just grab me a tissue, love,' I added to Mike.

'You *sure*?' said John, clearly concerned.

'Sure I'm sure,' I said. 'It's just ... oh, God, John,' I said, sighing, 'I've still got his mobile. So we've been through it – you know, just to try and get a sense of what happened – and there were lots of texts beforehand, between him and Cameron, and – oh, John, it would break your heart. Texts asking Tyler to see if he could sneak out and join them – this Cameron, and the two boys I'd seen Tyler with earlier. I feel so bad for him, John. I know exactly why he's in the state he is. He'd texted back – and more than once, too – saying no. Saying he was tired ... saying he didn't want to get into any more trouble ... And then there's a final one, which he ignored, and I bet that's been eating him up. So I know *exactly* how he's feeling now. Bloody wretched.'

'Oh, Casey,' John said, 'that's just so bloody awful. Jesus – I can't imagine what he's going through – and what about you two? You must be feeling so strung out. How are you holding up?'

'We're still a bit numb, I think,' I told him. 'Tyler's fast asleep – they gave him something at the hospital and we have more for tonight. But I'm dreading him waking up, if I'm honest with you. I really am.'

'Well, I'll come over then, Casey,' he said straight away. 'It's no trouble. I'm sure all Tyler needs from you now is support – and I know you'll be able to give him that, but maybe if I sat down with him, encouraged him to talk to me … would that be helpful? Or maybe if I got hold of Will? What d'you think would be best? My only concern – and it's not a huge one – is that it might agitate him to see either of us … I don't know. What d'you think? As I say, I'm happy to jump in the car. Just say.'

He'd actually made a point – something I'd not properly thought of. He was right. Knowing Tyler, it would make things worse, giving him an opportunity to retreat and bottle up his feelings. And that wouldn't help at all – in fact it would really set us back. No, we needed to deal with this ourselves, no doubt about it. But just getting it off my chest had helped enormously, I realised. No, we'd be okay. We had to be, didn't we?

I didn't know what to expect to happen when Tyler woke up, but if I'd been asked to guess it would never have occurred to me that he'd just appear in the living room, mid-afternoon, seemingly out of nowhere and wrapped up in his duvet. Well, the pink duvet, which felt incongruous and way too bright and cheerful under the circumstances, and only served to highlight just how shattered and pale he looked.

I leapt from the chair – we'd been watching some chat show from way down the listings – went across to him and herded him across to the sofa. 'Oh, sweetheart,' I said, 'come on, get yourself settled down here, while I get you something to eat and drink. You must be starving.'

Tyler didn't answer. He just sat down on the sofa, as directed, swinging his legs up so he was lying along it. He looked cocooned, wrapped up sausage-roll style, with just his head sticking out. I suspected the drugs had really knocked him for six. Not to mention the bump and cuts on the back of his head.

Mike followed me into the kitchen. 'I'm not sure he's going to want to eat anything, Case, love.'

'Oh, I know,' I said, because I'd realised it too. 'Just instinctive, I guess. I'll make him a sandwich anyway. And he needs a drink at least.'

Mike squeezed my shoulder. 'Whatever you say, love.'

By the time I followed Mike back into the living room, Tyler seemed sleepy again, leading me to wonder if he'd actually come down in a kind of sleepwalk. But when I perched at the end of the sofa by his feet, he stirred. He was facing the sofa back and I could see that his eyes were now fully open, and he was just lying there, staring at the fabric.

'Love,' I said gently, 'do you want to talk about it? You know, if you talk about it – how you're feeling – it might help make it a little better.'

There was a long silence, then he turned and eased himself up slightly. 'How can anything make it better? Cam's dead, and it's my fault.'

'Your fault?' I looked across at Mike and back to Tyler. 'Love, it's not your fault. Why on earth would you think that?'

'Course it is. Read my phone if you don't believe me. They wanted me to go with them. My mates. To meet Cam and his other mates. And I said no, because I couldn't. And now Cam's dead. Simple.'

Mike got up from the armchair and went over to kneel in front of Tyler. 'Listen, mate,' he said. 'No matter what you think, I know better. It's *not* your fault. You did right not to go with them. If you had, there might have been four of you in that car.'

'No!' Tyler said, his voice rising. 'If I'd been there they wouldn't have even nicked a car in the first place. I know they wouldn't. We'd have just stayed round the old estate or something, I know we would.'

'You don't know that, mate,' Mike said softly. 'None of us do. What I do know was that this was a tragic accident that never should have happened. No kid should lose his life that way, but this is *not* down to you. You shouldn't have been out with them and you knew that, and I, for one, am very glad you weren't.' He ran a hand across Tyler's fore-head. '*Very* glad, son. Okay? Because it might just have saved *your* life.'

Watching Mike speaking to him so tenderly made me fill up all over again, but it was Tyler's tears that plopped onto the duvet. 'Why, Mike?' he sobbed. 'Why did he have to die on me? He's my best mate. He's the only one who knows what it's like to be me.' He burrowed down into the duvet and started sobbing all over again. And what could we say to make the pain better for him? Nothing?

To my relief, however, he was asleep again within minutes, and while he retreated into welcome oblivion we retreated into the kitchen.

'God!' said Mike, banging his fist down on the worktop. He cleared his throat then, noisily, as he plucked up the kettle.

He was too choked up to speak. And I was as well.

The death of a young person is never less than tragic. It just goes against the natural order of everything. And the ripples that spread from it would travel far and very widely, and they could, I knew, soon engulf Tyler. They already had, really – they had him in their grip and were threatening to drown him. And we had to address that – though I didn't think we could do that ourselves. He needed professional targeted help to see him through what must have felt like the end of the world for him, and my first job, once the world of work was back in its collective office, was to get in touch with John again and see to it that he got some.

There was no question of him going into school. Even had he wanted to, I knew he was far too emotionally fragile; not to mention the small matter of what must be an extremely sore head. Though, bless him, when I looked in on him after Mike had left for work on the Monday morning, his face told me he'd been expecting me to send him.

His chin wobbled right away, in fact, just as soon as he saw me. 'Please don't make me go to school, Casey,' he said. '*Please*. I just can't face them all. Can't face Grant, can't face my mates, can't face the teachers. I just can't bear them asking me stuff,' he finished, tears rolling down his cheeks.

'You don't have to go into school, love,' I reassured him. 'You're not ready for that yet. No, you stay in bed. I just came in to see if you thought you could eat something. Can I tempt you with a bacon sandwich? Some cereal? Some toast?'

It had been a long time since he'd eaten anything of any substance, only picking at tea the previous evening, too choked with grief to swallow, and it had crossed my mind – in fact, it had crossed both our minds – if we should get back in touch with John and have him pass the news on to his father; perhaps a text or call from him, or if not from him, at least from his brother, might provide him with a much-needed shred of comfort.

But instinct had told me otherwise. Would they even care? Yes, they might feel a modicum of sadness – what thinking, feeling human being wouldn't? – but I suspected there would be a lack of real feeling behind it, and the last thing Tyler needed was to have all that emotion – all that hope for his family – stirred up, only to have them fade away into the distance again.

'I'm not very hungry,' he said now. 'I'm just tired.'

'I'm not surprised, love,' I said, giving his arm a squeeze. 'Not with what you've been through. And the doctors gave you some strong medicine to help you sleep properly so that your head can heal up. You go back to sleep, sweetheart. I'll come back and look in on you in an hour or so, but just shout if you need me, okay?'

'I wish I could sleep,' he said. 'But my brain just won't let me. I keep remembering everything … I can't believe I'm never going to see him again.'

I put my arm around him. 'Oh, love,' I said. 'I know. Look, if you don't want to be on your own, how about we set you up down on the sofa?'

But he shook his head. 'Maybe if I could just have the TV on quietly?'

'That's a good idea,' I said. 'Let's find you something nice and distracting, eh?'

I picked up the remote, changing the channel even as I took it off standby. The last thing I wanted to flash up was the usual fare of the main channels early on a weekday morning – it would be news, and odds on, the majority of it would be bad. Which was fine, of course – till it had already hit you square in the eye.

Once downstairs my first plan had been to call John back again, but the phone started ringing as I approached it. It was Will, who'd caught up with my message and who'd also been brought up to speed by John.

He came straight to the point. 'Is there anything you need from me, Casey? I'll be over as soon as you think it's appropriate, but in the meantime what can I do to help?'

My thoughts were already centred on the Child and Adolescent Mental Health Service, who seemed the best port of call in the short term. 'Can you look into some kind of bereavement counselling for him, do you think, Will? I'm sure CAMHS will have something they could set up for him, won't they?'

'Of course,' Will said. 'And I'll get onto that right away. I'm not sure how soon it can happen, though. Just to make you aware, the waiting list is pretty long at the moment, but, I tell you what – I'll look into a couple of other organisations; there are bound to be some local to you that can perhaps do something faster. Anything else?'

'I'm not sure right now,' I said. 'It's all happened so quickly, we're in a bit of a daze, still. I just have this sense that we need to get on top of things, that we need to act quickly. I don't know why, but I just have this horrible feeling that he might try to do something to hurt himself, you know?'

'Absolutely,' Will said. 'The poor lad's had so much to deal with these past few months, and I completely agree – straws and camels' backs – this is the sort of thing that could so easily tip him over the edge. Bad enough for any kid, having something like this happen, but in Tyler's circumstances the potential rises exponentially. Leave it with me. Let's get him a counsellor. And, as I say, I'll be round myself – probably tomorrow, if that suits, but definitely by Wednesday. But in the meantime it's really a case of you and Mike keeping a close eye on him; keep the lines of communication open … but I'm teaching my granny to suck eggs, aren't I? You know what to do. Er …' he paused. 'Not that I'm in any way likening you to a granny, of course …'

'Will,' I pointed out. 'I *am* a granny. Three times over, remember? And, well, thanks. I really appreciate it. Thanks a mill.'

* * *

I phoned school straight after speaking to Will, to explain both what had happened, and that Tyler wouldn't be coming in for a few days. And it was only after I'd spoken to them that it really hit me how little we knew about the lad who was so dear to our little man.

And when I put the phone down it was to find the little man himself standing in the doorway, in his favourite Spiderman pyjamas and the red fleecy dressing gown we'd bought for him. He looked hollow eyed – so young and frail and so, so sad.

'Casey,' he said in a small voice, 'can I ask you something?'

I hurried over to him. 'Come on, sweetie,' I said, 'on the couch with you. And yes, of course you can. You can ask me anything. What do you want to ask?'

'It's just that I was watching Jeremy Kyle upstairs,' he said, as I got him settled and reached for the TV remote for him. 'Did I ever tell you? That was my mum's favourite programme.'

'No, you didn't, love,' I said, worrying that he was watching something so volatile. But perhaps the routine slanging matches and shouting were the sort of distraction that suited him best. And who was I to judge anyway?

'Was it, sweetie?' I said.

'The social worker who used to come and see me at Dad's told me that. She used to know my mum, see. That's how she knew stuff like that.'

I waited for him to continue, wondering where this might be leading. 'What about it, love?' I coaxed when he didn't answer.

'Well, it was just that I was watching it,' he said finally, 'and the lady that was on there just now, well, her mum died and she was sad because she couldn't have a proper funeral because they never found her, so she couldn't say goodbye to her …'

'Oh dear,' I said, wondering what terrible circumstances had been involved. Was that really the best thing for him to have been looking at? Apparently so.

'Well, it was just, like, I wondered. Cam'll have a funeral, won't he? Like a proper one?'

'Of course he will,' I said.

'So would you take me?' he asked me. 'So I can say goodbye to him properly?'

I perched at the end of the sofa, thinking fast before answering his question, because I didn't want to promise him something I couldn't deliver. Would social services be happy for me to take him, given his age and the circumstances? I thought they probably would, but having never been in this position before I couldn't really guarantee it till I'd checked with John.

But something told me I was on safe ground. On what grounds would they refuse it? Cameron was Tyler's closest friend; what could be inappropriate about taking him to say goodbye? However harrowing it might be – and I knew it would be that – if he wanted to go, it would be wrong to refuse it. In fact, if they did, I'd put my case till I could make them see reason. No, it would be fine. And yes, I'd take him.

'I will, love,' I said. 'We'll go together and we'll take some flowers. We'll say a proper goodbye to Cameron.

We'll be there, I promise. He was your best friend and it's important that you're there for him, isn't it?'

Tyler nodded and smiled, albeit infinitesimally. But it was like a sun shaft coming down, even so.

Chapter 17

As I'd suspected, John agreed to Tyler attending Cameron's funeral, but almost as soon as I put the phone down I felt an unexpected wave of anxiety, bordering on mild dread. Yes, I'd always known I'd have to steel myself for the business of supporting Tyler through it. He was so young and so fragile, and it would be extremely traumatic for him. But it hadn't really hit me before now that it would be so traumatic for me too.

I had never before been to the funeral of someone so young, and I had no idea what to expect. All I had to go on was my instinct as a mother, doing that thing that every parent can't help but do from time to time, trying to imagine the unimaginable: how on earth I would go on if it was one of my own children who had died.

I was genuinely shocked by how upset I was by thoughts of Cameron's mother and how on earth she was currently getting through each day. But then maybe it was inevitable; I knew this funeral would be unlike any funeral I'd been to before; knew I would have to be braced for the sheer punch-in-the-gut emotion of it all. Yes, this was going to be tough, no question. He'd been 15 years old. It was so wrong, so unfair. So distressing.

Mike had more prosaic concerns. 'I'm going to take a day's leave,' he said, once Tyler had spoken to his friend James, and we'd established that it would take place the following Monday. 'I think I should be there. Emotions can run pretty high at funerals,' he pointed out, 'and I don't doubt there will be lots of the lad's friends there.'

'There's no need, love,' I said, conscious that annual leave days weren't in unlimited supply. 'We'll be okay. What could possibly happen?'

'Probably nothing,' he said, 'but I'd feel much happier being there, even so. Just in case anything kicks off – just in case things get volatile, that's all.'

It was something that hadn't occurred to me and it provided a new source of worry. Though logic told me that as Cameron had been the one behind the wheel, the family and friends of the other boys would have no axe to grind – he'd driven the car and he'd been the one to pay the price, hadn't he? But Mike was right – we didn't know everything, and the situation might have been more complex. There was always the possibility that it had been one of the other boys who'd instigated the plan, wasn't there? And though my instinct was to shy away from even thinking what it must feel like to lose your child, I couldn't help thinking of Cameron's mum and what she must be going through right now. How was she going to get through the day?

No, I was grateful Mike would be there. He would also be a great support to Tyler. More than perhaps I'd even realised in the past few months, there was this connection between them now that was something really special.

Monday dawned and I opened the curtains to grey skies and drizzle. Fitting, yes, but at the same time so depressing. Just another shade of grey to add to the darkness of the occasion, and as we drove to the outskirts of town, where the crematorium and cemetery were, we couldn't escape the date either. It was just two days before Halloween and didn't we know it.

Once just the support act that happened before the big occasion of Bonfire Night, Halloween had changed beyond recognition since I was a child, and had kicked Guy Fawkes and fireworks into touch. Now it was all about the undead and was something of a freak-show, and it didn't escape my notice how many houses were already decorated with cardboard ghouls and ghosts and RIP headstones.

I turned to look at Tyler, who was wiping the condensation from the car window – was he taking in the irony of it, too?

I felt a rush of love for him; he looked so vulnerable sitting there in his new black suit and snowy-white shirt, his normally unruly mop of hair wrestled into sleek order – combed down over the shaved patch and bruising and stitches – and his school shoes polished to an almost patent shine.

These were the important human rituals, the marks of love and respect to the departed, and going through them with him had been cathartic. Now he looked the part as well as felt it; his face pinched, his expression scared and anxious. Every inch the sad child *en route* to a funeral.

'You okay, sweetheart?' I asked him. 'You sure you're still up for doing this? It's not too late to change your mind if you need to. No one would blame you if you decided you couldn't face it, love. You can say goodbye in other ways if you'd prefer. Funerals are never nice.'

He already knew this to some extent as Mike and I had spent much of the week preparing him. From taking him to get the cheap suit in Asda, to explaining the logistics of the service and cremation, we'd done as much as we could to minimise the shock factor on the day. Even so, I knew he *would* be shocked. How could he not be? It was something that would stay with him for life.

'I'm okay,' he said firmly. 'I want to go. I want to be there for Cam so's he knows I care.'

And there was no arguing with that one. So we didn't.

The crematorium and cemetery were in a beautiful setting, reached by a long, winding drive which was flanked by woodland. The trees had all but lost their leaves now and instead sent a lacework of bare branches up into the sky which, silhouetted, were equally beautiful in their way. There was also a river running through, today a glossy charcoal ribbon, which added to the sense that this was a place of peace.

I'd last been here not long ago, as it happened, when an elderly neighbour of my parents had passed away, back in the summer. I hadn't known him that well, but I'd stepped in as chauffeur for the day, taking my dad and two friends – none of them drove themselves any more – so they could pay their respects.

And that was what it had been about – paying respects – as well as celebrating a long life, well lived. Yes, there were tears, of course there were, but there was also acceptance. There would be no acceptance at Cameron's funeral – how could there be?

The crematorium itself sat amid huge formal displays of roses and other shrubs and flowers, their growth presumably aided by the ashes of many, many souls. It felt like a macabre thing to be thinking, but it was strangely apt, even so. Ashes to ashes. That was the fate of us all ultimately.

But too soon in this case, I thought, as we drove past the crematorium and on to the little chapel where the service was to be held. And it was brought home to me by the mass of young people who were clustered there; their sheer numbers feeling so out of place at *any* funeral – typically the preserve of the mostly adult and elderly.

As we swung into the car park I could see that well over half the mourners were teenagers, a few of the lads dressed in suits, like Tyler, but many others in jeans and trackies, as I'd expected.

'Can I go and say hello to my mates?' Tyler asked as we all climbed out of the car and I wrestled with the catch on my umbrella. People were now beginning to file in but the rain had got heavier, and with the log-jam at the entrance I wondered if the chapel would even be able to hold us all.

'Course you can, son,' Mike told him. 'But wait by the door for us, okay? So we can all go in together.'

Nowhere to Go

I had wondered before if Tyler would ask to sit with his friends, but he didn't. And I was glad. It felt important that we were both right beside him.

I watched him run across, and, somewhat bizarrely, found myself worrying about him getting muddy water on his trousers, as he paid no attention to the puddles he was running through. How stupid, I mentally chastised myself.

'Let's give him a few minutes, shall we?' I said to Mike, finally able to cover us both with the brolly, and managing to poke him in the cheek in the process. He took it from me – in umbrella terms, our height difference was a bit of a nightmare – and he tutted as he agreed. 'Case, love, it's a funeral, not a fashion show,' he said, but gave my shoulder a supporting squeeze, even so.

We went across to the chapel entrance, where it looked like we'd just be able to squeeze in, though there was no chance of us getting a seat. Which was fine. In some ways it felt appropriate to be standing at a time like this.

We called Tyler over to us as the last stragglers entered, and as he walked across I felt glad we'd let him come and be with his friends. 'I think he'll be okay, you know,' Mike whispered, reading my thoughts. 'I think this might do him good, being here.'

I hoped so. Hoped so much, but how could we know yet? For all the trauma of today, the *real* hard part was what came next.

The service was heart-breaking, in the true sense of the word. Well, as close you could get to it without actually dying, I thought, as I watched the young woman at the front – clearly Cameron's mother – having to be physically held up by two teenage boys.

Heart-breaking. There was no other word for it. From the coffin, which was white and was just short of being adult-sized, to the haunting, keening sound of mass crying. To know that the body that lay in the box on which all our eyes were fixed was that of an adolescent, not even fully grown before being taken – no, I hadn't known him, but I felt that grief myself.

He was loved – that much was clear. And this was the place to express it. And *only* it – no recriminations, no blame, no sense of waggling, hectoring, lecturing fingers. Love was all that mattered now, it was clear.

It was funny being at the funeral of someone I barely knew, though, Mike and I standing among a congregation of complete strangers. I felt slightly detached, and though that meant I didn't feel the visceral pain of those who had known him, Tyler included, what I felt in its place was almost as intense; an objective sense of the depth of the grief I was seeing, from the elderly couple – possibly his grandparents? – who were trying so hard to maintain their composure, to the teenaged friends who were wailing loudly and unashamedly – staggered beyond reason by this cruel intrusion of death into their young lives. They clung to one another, literally, holding each other up, and it was so plain to see how they simply couldn't process the knowledge that they would never see their friend again.

I could see Tyler feeling it, too. The tears ran unchecked down his face, which was contorted as if in agony as he tried to take in what he was seeing and hearing; chiefly the horrible, horrible pain of all his friends. And when the service finished and it was time to make our way to the crematorium I leaned towards him. 'Go and be with them,' I told him. 'Walk up there with them. We'll be right behind you.' I hugged him. 'Go on, go.'

He took my forearm in both his hands and then he squeezed it. 'Are you okay?' he asked. And I realised he was referring to my own tears, which were still spilling over my cheeks.

It stunned and moved me to see the concern in his eyes. 'I'll be fine, love,' I said, hugging him. 'You go on.'

I looked at Mike then and I could see he was beyond words himself. There *were* no words, really. Not one.

If the service had been gruelling, the cremation itself was even worse, and words are not sufficient to explain what that day did to me. It wasn't about me – far from it – but I defy any thinking, feeling person not to be affected, and on a very deep level, by the ritual of death as played out with the very young. My next clear memory was of the coffin finally leaving us. Of it moving off, behind the velvet curtains, accompanied by a haunting, beautiful song called *White Flag*, by Dido, and of what remained – a large framed photograph of a 15-year-old boy, smiling out at our stricken faces, as if to demand that we remember him as he was: so cute, so good-looking, so full of life.

I tugged at Mike's sleeve then. I had to get out of there.

Outside, I knew it would only be a matter of minutes before everyone joined us. Specifically, Tyler, who I needed to be strong for. This was tragic, but, strictly speaking, it wasn't our tragedy. I needed to leave the mourners and be by myself for a bit, so I could compose myself, blow my nose and wipe away the tears. 'I need to go and sit in the car for a bit,' I said to Mike, 'if you don't mind waiting here for Tyler. No rush. He'll want to say goodbye to his friends, won't he?'

Thankfully, Mike understood. I knew he wouldn't want me standing in the rain waiting for the next wave of distress. He gave me the car keys and I hurried off gratefully.

It must have been ten or 15 minutes but it felt like only moments had passed before I heard the back door of the car open.

I swivelled round. It was Tyler, holding the order of service pamphlet over his head, as if it might in some small way protect him from the lashing rain. He clambered in, looking pale but dry-eyed now, thank God.

'No Mike, love?' I asked him, there having been no corresponding clunk of the driver's door.

He shook his head. 'He met someone. Some friend of his. From another funeral, I think.'

As would be expected. Funerals were a business and a production line, like anything else.

'So I thought I'd come back and see if you're okay,' he added. 'Are you all right?'

I reassured him that I was. 'But I think I need a hug,' I said, opening my own door and clambering back out so I could climb into the back seat beside him.

'More to the point,' I asked as I drew him close to me and we settled back into the seat, 'are *you* okay?'

He considered for a moment, as I rested my chin on the top of his head. His hair felt soft and smelt of our coconut shampoo. 'I'm better now,' he said at length. 'Now it's over. And you know what's funny?'

'What's funny?'

'I just kept on thinking about my mum. You know, while it was all going on, all the singing and praying? I just kept thinking how my mum never had that, like on Jeremy Kyle, like I said to you? It was like, so *weird*, it was like I was saying goodbye to her too. And, like, I dunno, like he was going off to be with her. That she knew he was my best friend so she was up in the sky waiting for him, you know?'

'Yes, I know exactly what you mean, love.'

I found myself smiling as I followed his thought process. *Yes.* I didn't know how he'd got that, but he'd *got* that. Made the link between the two significant deaths in his young life, and it had brought him comfort. I kissed the top of his head.

'I know *exactly* what you mean,' I said again. 'And that's a good way to think about it, isn't it? That she'll be there to greet him, ready to say hello.'

'An' he can tell her how I'm doing, can't he?'

'Yes, love, he definitely can.'

We were silent for a few minutes then, and in the silence I had a thought. 'Tyler?' I asked him. 'You know, your mum *would* have had a funeral. Do you know what happened when she died? Was she buried or cremated? Has anyone ever told you?'

I felt him shake his head. 'I don't know,' he said. 'I don't even know where she went. I was shipped off to my dad's and I was still only a baby, really. I don't remember hardly anything about any of it.'

I paused a heartbeat before speaking. Was this a good thing to do? 'And would you *like* to know, love?' I asked him anyway. 'You know, find out where she went, where her funeral was? Because I could try for you. Could try and find out where the funeral was, and we could, oh, I don't know, take her a letter, take some flowers …'

He looked up at me. 'And say hello? Actually, goodbye,' he corrected himself. 'Could you? D'you really think you could do that?'

'Well, I can't promise,' I said, 'but I could certainly speak to John about it for you. There'll be some records somewhere, I'm sure.'

He wriggled free of me then, sitting up straight, sideways on to me. 'An' you know what else we could do? We could take Billy Bear.'

'Billy Bear?'

'When I went to my dad's I had this blue teddy, called Billy. It was in my cot, they said – you know, when they found me and everything? So the social people brought it, like with the photo.'

'The photo you brought with you to us?' I asked.

He nodded. 'My mum had that in her purse. They took that, too. Anyway, they took them to my dad's for me. I had the photo stuck on my wall – that's how it broked, when I ripped it off there – and I used to take Billy to bed every night. An' then, when I got too old for it, I hid it in the cupboard in our bedroom. Grant could get it for me, couldn't he?' he said. 'Couldn't he? They would've taken it when they moved, wouldn't they? And we could take that when we go there. That way, she'll know it's me come to see her, won't she?'

How I managed not to fall apart hearing that, I'll never know. Perhaps put it down to a strenuous wish not to be self-indulgent, not in the face of such a thing on such a day. Thankfully Mike arrived back at the car almost at that moment, so we were able to move on to the fact that he'd met up with a former work colleague whose mother had died. And as we drove out – I stayed in the back – I held Tyler's hand tightly, feeling lighter of heart about him than I had in the whole time we'd had him, knowing this could be the key that unlocked a brighter future for him, and that I suddenly held it in my hand.

And I would. This was something tangible I could do, and I would. If I couldn't actually *be* his mum, at least I could be the one to find her.

Chapter 18

When I was a young girl, my absolute favourite pastime was reading. I loved stories, I loved books, I loved disappearing into them, and would enjoy nothing more than to lose myself for hours in a fantasy world, where I would naturally become one of the main characters.

My speciality was always the same one: doing good, fighting evil and putting the world to rights generally. I remember glancing up one day, from my usual position curled up on the sofa, surprised to find my mum was also in the room with me, along with two of the neighbours. And they'd been there, chatting away over tea and cake, for quite a while.

'Look at her,' Mum had laughed, 'completely oblivious to the real world. You know, Casey, if you're not careful you're going to turn into one of those characters. One day I'll come in and you'll have been swallowed up into the pages.' And she made a sucking sound – swoosh! – and there I was, gone.

And, oh, how I'd wished she was right, and it could happen. I loved my mum and dad and my life and my sister, but, oh, how the thought of that had thrilled me. I so wanted to be just like Nancy Drew (as a girl, Carolyn Keene was my favourite, favourite author) or George, from The Famous Five, with my faithful dog, Timmy. Someone who always knew just what to do in order to make everything right.

That's just how I felt now, I realised. That I was on a very important mission. Only this time it would be one without lashings of lemonade and faithful dogs – this was to be one in which the characters were real people, and where the ending hadn't already been written.

And even though that meant I might be on a hiding to nothing, I was confident. And I was also excited. I could only see good coming from this. I just knew that if I could reunite Tyler and his mother (even if it was going to have to be from beyond the grave) it would be the start of a healing process for him.

Within a few days, I was well under way, too. I had by now been given copies of all Tyler's records; a mixture of original copies of all new and recent documents, as well as historical files which would have included every piece of paperwork from the day he was found with his mother's body and through the process of him being placed with his dad. The case was closed shortly afterwards, once social services were satisfied about his well-being, so there was a gap before the more recent tranche of paperwork, when the case was re-opened following the knife incident in the spring.

I had everything spread out on the dining table now, and I was busy poring over every word while Tyler was upstairs having a bath. We'd not long finished dinner and Mike was sitting opposite me, helping himself to bubble and squeak – we'd had it for tea with some sausages and there was still plenty left in the pan. 'Waste not, want not,' he chirped as he scooped a spoonful onto his plate. 'Quick, while Miss Marple over there isn't looking,' he added, pretending to be talking to himself.

I laughed and put down the file I was currently reading. 'I can see you, love. I'm simply choosing to ignore you. Have all you like. It's your waistline after all.'

I picked the file up again and sighed, glancing towards my mobile. 'I wish Will would phone,' I said. 'It's been days. Or was I supposed to be calling him? I can't remember if I was meant to ring him. Do you think it's too late to give him a quick call now?'

I had spoken to both Will and John the day after the funeral and told them of my plans to track down Tyler's birth mother. Will had been really positive, too – all for it, in fact. And right away promised to try and do some digging. 'His dad *must* know,' he reasoned. 'They were bound to have told him where she was buried – or where her ashes were scattered – because there would have been a presumption that they might like to take Tyler to visit, wouldn't there? If I'd been the mother's social worker, I'd have expected that. And it doesn't really matter that he had nothing to do with her by that point, because it would have been done in the interest of the child.'

When I spoke to John, on the other hand, I got slightly less enthusiasm for my endeavours. But I suppose I'd expected that even before I made the call.

'It's just I'm not sure it's our remit to do this, Casey,' he pointed out. 'Whatever good it might do, it's also opening a new can of worms, and we have no way of knowing what the repercussions might be. It could be that rather than closing a book, it's opening a new one, with all the attendant upset and potential for hurt. Which is fine – if it ultimately leads to closure for him, but to do this right now? Is this really the best time? When everything else in his life's up in the air?'

'But is there *going* to be a better time to do this?' I asked.

'Yes,' John replied, very firmly. 'The best time to do it, to my mind, is when his future is more settled – that's the time to start digging in the past. When he's placed long term, say, and he's settled and has the future mapped out a bit. Or, if that's the way things pan out, when he's back with his father.'

I noticed the 'father' rather than the 'parents' and I pounced on it.

'You really, honestly think that that might still be a possibility, John? Because I don't. Not for a second. She's wanted him gone from the outset – that was why she pressed charges over the knife thing. And I've seen nothing since to make me think his dad is even trying to change her mind. So she's got what she wants, hasn't she? She's even tried to turn his brother against him. I think there's as much chance of him going home as the proverbial pig taking wing, that's what I think.'

'I know,' John said. 'I know. You're probably right. But even so …'

'And have you any sighting of a long-term family on the horizon yet?' I asked him, unwilling to concede now that I had the bit so firmly in my teeth.

Again, a negative. Yes, it seemed the wheels were well in motion, but placements for 12-year-old boys with a record of aggression weren't generally many to the pound.

'So there might not be a good time any time soon,' I persisted. 'And it's not as if I have to share anything I find with Tyler unless and until we all agree it's something we should share. How about that?'

At which point he held his hands up – we were on the phone, but he made a point of telling me he was doing it – and agreed that I could give it a go.

But that had been a few days ago now and so far I'd heard nothing. Not from John – though I wasn't expecting to – and not from Will either.

Mike looked at me now. 'Casey, you know as well as I do that Will told you to give him a few days. And that as soon as he knew anything he'd ring *you*. And in answer to your question, yes, it *is* too late to ring him anyway. So you'll just need to be patient for a bit longer.'

Which left me in limbo, which was not a place I wanted to be. Because no matter how carefully and thoroughly I had scrutinised the files, I hadn't been able to find any clues that would lead me to Fiona's final resting place. Which I could understand. With everything else going on – the key thing being having a three-year-old apparently orphaned

– it wasn't surprising that his then social worker hadn't made a note saying, 'Oh, yes, and the mother's buried at …' And I knew there might be a good reason for that, too – mother and son might have had separate social workers. There might have been a more long-standing one, whose remit was to take care of Fiona herself, and a new one, brought in during the pregnancy possibly, whose sole responsibility was to Tyler. And when and if it did come up – say, Tyler's father had asked in passing – it would probably be the sort of detail that would have been passed on vocally.

And, in that regard, I could only hope Will had had more luck. I knew from John, who'd already spoken to him by the time he'd spoken to me, that Will had at least made an appointment to pop round and see them. And, as Mike had pointed out, all I could do while that happened was be patient, and, because I did value John's wisdom and saw the rationale behind his reticence, try to keep a lid on Tyler's hopes as well.

Tyler had gone back to school the previous morning and seemed, so far, to have got on okay. We'd kept him off for a couple of days after the funeral, which felt the right thing to do, both because of his emotional fragility and to allow his head wound to heal a bit – and he certainly couldn't do PE for a while yet. But it was important to get him back into school and bonding with his peer group; he would heal mentally just as quickly there as he would at home, and I knew the distraction of school would be good for him.

We'd also talked a little more about the teddy bear.

'Why did you feel you were too big to take him to bed with you?' I asked him, while we cleared the tea things the night before his return to school. It was a little detail that had been on my mind since he'd told me about it. He couldn't have been more than ten or so at the time – perhaps younger – and when I remembered back to Kieron and his friends, those notions of things 'being babyish' didn't kick in till much later.

'Cos of Alicia, of course,' he said, but almost matter of factly, which was encouraging. 'She was always telling me I was pathetic to have a teddy bear.'

'But what about Grant? Didn't he have a teddy bear?'

'Course he did. But he was younger, weren't he? An' I know she just used to do it to wind me up, like everything else. Like she'd tell me she'd have him off me and put him in the charity bag when I was in school. So I hid him away.' He shrugged. 'Seemed safest.'

'And then forgot all about him when you moved?'

He shook his head. 'Nah, I didn't forget him,' he said defensively. 'Well, I s'pose I kind of did,' he admitted, 'what with moving into the new house and everything. But he should be there somewhere, shouldn't he? But don't ask *her*, ask Grant,' he added, suddenly anxious. 'She'll say she can't find him and then bin him just to be horrible,' he said.

And, sadly, I suspected he might be right. 'Well,' I said, ruffling his hair, 'we'll have to keep our fingers crossed, won't we? But even if we can't track Billy down, we can buy your mum a new teddy, how about that? Because, to be honest, love, she won't mind at all. Shall I tell you something about mums, Tyler? They watch over you, always. Whether they're there or they're not there, whether they're alive or they're gone – that's what they do – they watch over you for ever.'

'You know Cam?' he said, which broke my heart – as if I could ever forget him. 'He told me that as well. He said his mum told him that when his nan died. She had a star and everything. He showed me once. She's on the handle of the saucepan. She was good at soup,' he added, by way of explanation.

Call it the saucepan, call it the plough, call it anything you wanted, but there was something in the constellations that was in the right place, clearly, because finally, by that Friday afternoon, the one just after Firework Night, my patience was rewarded.

Tyler had gone off to school full of excitement about the secret place we were taking him after school that day. And as I waved him off it occurred to me that in the past couple of weeks we'd seen not an inkling of the behaviours that had been responsible for him coming to us; that he had – for the moment anyway, in the midst of all this trauma – become a markedly different boy. He'd yet to reach adolescence, yes, and there would be challenges ahead for whoever ended up providing a home for him – I didn't doubt that. But, for the moment, he was (to use the holy-grail adage) no trouble at all. So much so, that the only reason I was paying much attention to his chart was because he was keen to earn his points, finish paying my dad's tenner back and get enough together to buy credit for his phone.

I went back into the kitchen and looked at it now, at all the completed pages filled with ticks, held together with a fat bulldog clip, all bristling with different-coloured page separators. They were evidence that he had moved through all the various levels he'd needed to in order to complete the programme. He was the first kid we'd had in ages who'd completed the entire process and I felt so proud of how he'd managed to achieve that. Soon, the pages would have a golden top sheet, signed off by John Fulshaw himself (which always thrilled the children no end) after which he'd be awarded a formal certificate which would be presented to him at a celebratory party.

But that was something to think about in a couple of weeks rather than now. Right now we were off to Riley's and I was really looking forward to it. After the emotional intensity of the previous week it would be a tonic, I knew, just to have a glass of something in one hand and a sparkler in the other, going *wheee!* with Tyler and the grandkids. She'd kindly invited us all round to her house, where David was going to put on a firework display and a bit of a bonfire, while she and I were in charge of jacket potatoes, pie and peas and – the *pièce de resistance* – my homemade ginger cake with toffee sauce. I was just about to get out my baking apron when the phone rang.

'Oh hi, John,' I said when I realised who it was. 'Have you got some news for me?'

'Indeed I have,' was the response, and I noticed his gleeful tone. 'And you might want to sit down while I tell you all about it. It's quite a story, actually.'

Intrigued, I took myself and my mobile into the dining room and sat at the table. 'Ooh,' I said. 'Do go on.'

And what a story it turned out to be, as well as exactly the kind of news I'd been hoping for. It turned out that Will, despite his silence, had been quite relentless in his quest for knowledge about Tyler's mum. First off, he had been round to the Broughtons for the visit John had told me about, though on that occasion he'd been mostly rebuffed. No, they didn't know anything, and no, they didn't want to be involved in anything.

'Pretty much as predicted, then,' I noted.

'Yes, but then he had some success,' John went on, 'in that after what turned out to be quite a simple search through social services, he found out that Fiona had been cremated – a council-run, council-paid service and cremation, organised jointly by her old social worker and her drugs counsellor.'

John went on to tell me that Will also knew the whereabouts of her remains. Her ashes had apparently been scattered in a memorial garden in a crematorium just 25 miles away from us, in a small village close to where she'd died.

'Sounds positively sylvan,' I remarked.

'It does, doesn't it?' John agreed. 'But there are villages and there are villages, and I happen to know this one – and it's not very "escape to the country-esque". But the more interesting find –'

'There's more?' I asked excitedly.

'Yes indeed,' he said. 'It turns out that one of the permission forms – I think something to do with the hospital formally releasing the body – was signed by someone with the same surname as Fiona.'

'Really?' I could feel my investigator-gene kicking in now.

'Yes, and of course Will assumed at first that it might be a parent, now deceased. But he thought he'd check, so he trotted back round to the Broughtons where Tyler's father's reaction was apparently unexpected.'

'In what way? Why unexpected? What did he say, then?'

'Nothing. Just closed down. Gave Will the same story he had in the first place. That he didn't know anything about it –'

'But in such a way that made Will sure he did?'

'Got it in one. And also told him he should leave well alone.'

'Aha,' I said. 'Which would be like a red rag to a bull to me. So what happened next? Did Will press him?'

'Not right away. And then, just before Will had planned to call Tyler's dad again, he got a call in his office. From Alicia.'

He paused then. Probably to breathe, but the suspense was killing me. 'Go on then! Tell me, tell me!' I almost squealed at him.

'I'm trying to! And you won't believe what she told him – Fiona has a sister.'

'What?!' This was incredible news. 'How could no one have ever known that?'

'Half-sister,' John clarified. 'And very easily. I think the only reason it's come out now is because Alicia's seen an angle here. That the existence of this woman might well take the heat off them.'

Which, I thought sadly, really did put the lid on any notion that Tyler might ever be going back home again. But right now I was more interested in hearing about this sister whose existence had been unknown to social services. 'So what happened next?' I asked John.

'Will went back to speak to Tyler's father, obviously – just caught him, in fact, before he went back overseas. And it seems she's a good bit older than Fiona, and was – and still apparently is – a heroin addict too.'

'So he's still in touch with her?' I asked incredulously.

'No, he hasn't seen her since before Tyler was born but still occasionally hears tales *about* her, through an old school friend of his. Apparently she lives in a world where, if you get in debt with a dealer, you lose your legs, and the last contact he had with her – so he says, anyway – was just after he left Fiona and she threatened to have him "done over".'

'Wow!' I said. 'Who'd have thought it? So Tyler has an aunt. We know where his mum is, and he has an aunt!'

'Er, Casey,' John said, 'hold your horses. From all that – from all I've told you – the two snippets you comment on are that he has an aunt and we know the name of the chapel of rest? Did the rest go straight over your head? You know, the bit about the fact that his aunt is a hardened heroin addict? The fact that Alicia has all but admitted that she's washing her hands of Tyler? The bit about ...'

'No, no, of course not,' I said quickly. 'I twigged the Alicia bit straight away.'

I knew John was teasing me, but he was right, of course. All that other stuff wasn't as important to me right now as the fact that I had what I'd set out to find – a place where we could go and lay flowers for Tyler's mum. And, with luck, his old teddy as well. 'John, I heard it *all*,' I reassured him. 'And no doubt we'll have to revisit some of it, but bloody hell – what a turn-up, eh?'

'Well, yes, Casey, it is. But I'd go easy on the *we found you an aunt* bit if I were you. In fact, I'd counsel that you don't even mention it. From the sound of things, it's unlikely she'll remember anything about Tyler and his circumstances, and when I was talking about cans of worms the other day I meant it. We could have a found an enormous can of worms right there.'

'I know what you mean, John,' I said, 'and I agree absolutely – Tyler does not need another heroin addict in his life. But I'm thinking ahead here. I'm thinking about that long-term foster family. I just think that if he does have another living relative we'd be doing him a disservice if we didn't check it out. We owe him that much at least, don't we?'

I could hear John sigh at the end of the phone, but it was only a mildly exasperated sigh. 'Already in hand, Casey. In hand as we speak. Will has an address and I believe even a potential mobile phone number, with which – if it's the right one – he's currently trying to make contact. To see how she feels about it,' he added, 'which could go several ways. And one of them might involve the word "off".'

'But, equally, might not be,' I felt it was my duty to point out.

'And equally might not be,' John admitted.

It was very childish, but I did a Tyler and punched the air then. No, okay, so it hadn't been my own super-sleuth endeavours that had brought all this to light, but it *had* been me who had set the ball rolling in the first place, hadn't it? So I deserved at least a small pat on the back, didn't I? *Result*. I'd have something positive to share with Tyler at long last, and I couldn't have felt happier. So I punched the air again.

'But remember what I said,' John cautioned, having presumably read my mind. 'This *is* unlikely to be an aunt in the "remembering birthdays and bestowing unsolicited gifts" mould. So don't go off half-cocked and mention her to him, will you? Please don't risk getting his hopes up, not just yet.'

'As if I'd be that daft,' I reassured him. 'John, you know I wouldn't do that.'

'I know,' he chuckled. 'You're far too much the old pro. It's just that I can almost see the glint in your eye from down the phone line.'

And he was right there. He knew me too well.

Chapter 19

As I expected, Tyler was over the moon about the prospect of finally getting to say goodbye to his mum.

'Will it be a grave and stuff – so we can leave Billy there and everything? And I thought I could leave her a letter, as well, like I did for Grandad. She'd like that, wouldn't she?'

I was touched again by him calling my dad Grandad so naturally, and it plucked at my heartstrings. It wouldn't just be us who'd miss him when he'd left us. I also had to explain then what Will had told me. 'There won't be a grave, love,' I explained, 'because your mum was cremated, same as Cameron was. But Will's told me there is a cross for her, in a garden of remembrance. So hopefully we'll be able to leave Billy there.'

'And did Will ask Grant yet? You know, about getting Billy back for me?'

I bit my lip, wondering what to say. The truth was that Will had asked Tyler's dad about it, and had pretty much drawn a blank. He didn't know anything about any teddy apparently, nor where he might look for one, and though he promised he'd asked Grant if he knew anything about it, it brought it home to me – and saddened me – that something so important to the little boy, the son he'd taken in, could have passed through his life for several years without him even remembering. Just how often did that little boy ever get tucked into bed at night by his father? Just how often had he been given a goodnight kiss?

I tried to put it out of my mind. It was history. It couldn't be undone now. 'They've been looking,' I reassured him, realising I was probably lying. 'But you know what it's like when you move house, sweetheart. Lots of things get lost, and sometimes it takes years before they are found again. You watch. Just when they aren't looking for it, it will turn up, I'll bet. And, in the meantime, though, remember what I said? We'll go into town and get another bear, just like Billy. That way, if Billy does turn up, you still get to keep him as a memory. Then you and your mum will have one each, won't you? Just the same.'

Tyler processed what I'd told him and seemed to accept it. He smiled at me. 'That'll be nice. That's a good plan, Casey. It'll be like we have something together, won't it? When will we go?'

The village where the cemetery was was south of us, close to a city and, being a practical soul, I'd already figured that I could kill two birds with one stone. I'd never normally travel that far to shop, but since we'd be in the area anyway it was an opportunity for some serious retail therapy – just the antidote to what would be an emotional kind of day.

'Well,' I said to Tyler, 'I've been thinking about that, actually, and it'll soon be December, won't it? Time to start my Christmas shopping. So I thought that if we left it for a couple of weeks we could go into the big town centre there afterwards and you can help me choose some presents for the boys and Marley Mae. And also see the sort of thing you might like Santa to bring you, eh? What do you think?'

He was a boy, and had thus far shown little enthusiasm for shopping jaunts generally, but Christmas was Christmas, and the goal posts were therefore moved. He also vowed to be as good as gold until the big day arrived, of which I now had no doubt.

As far as Tyler's behaviours were concerned, progress continued to be promising. It was as if, after Cameron's death, he had changed overnight; as if he'd made a conscious choice to behave differently, as though some of his anger and frustration had died along with his friend. He was still as boisterous as ever, and still as sharp with his tongue when he chose, but that was a good thing – Mike and I could still see the essence of the real Tyler. Our job now was to build on that foundation so that when he left us to move to a more permanent home he would have all the tools he needed to live a fulfilling life.

Tyler was as good as his word, too. He was up on time for school every day, helpful with chores when he returned and, best of all, his progress at home seemed to be mirrored at school itself.

'It's like he's a different child,' his head of year told me when she phoned to report his weekly progress. This had been a regular thing since Tyler had moved up a level in his programme. It was a good way to check that the improvement was happening across the board. 'He's been a delight to teach,' she added. 'All his subject teachers have said so. Yes, he's had his sad time, understandably, but he's been so much less volatile, and, fingers crossed, relations with his brother seem better now as well.' This was particularly good to hear. So Alicia hadn't managed to completely turn Grant against him. 'That's great news,' I enthused. 'So they're speaking again?'

'They are. And in a healthy way. Tyler's not seeking him out so much. They often meet up at lunchtime, but it's not like it was. My spies tell me it's much as you'd expect it to be. Relaxed. None of that tension. So we're happy.'

I was happy, too. Even more so when I had a phone call from Will the following week telling me that he'd already been to see Tyler's aunt Angela.

'She's – how shall I put this politely?' Will said. 'Hmm. A bit of a rough old bird, I have to say.'

I laughed out loud. 'And does she cluck?'

'I couldn't imagine anyone *less* clucky,' he said. 'Don't worry – you'll know what I mean when you meet her.'

'When I *meet* her? Is she coming to visit, then?'

'Not exactly,' Will said. 'I don't think she's, ahem, really the "visiting" type. But she did say that she'd love to see Tyler, and though I can take him – and would be happy to – I thought you'd probably want to take him yourself, since it was you who instigated all of this. Anyway, so, being the presumptuous type, I told her I thought you'd probably be up for it.'

Up for it? He was right. I would have run over hot coals.
If she was dying to meet her nephew, then I was dying to
meet her. It would be lovely for Tyler to have another
family member in his life, even if she was a rough old bird.

'I understand you're going to see his mum's memory
cross too,' Will went on. 'I think that will be fantastic for
him, Casey. Give him something to hold on to, something
tangible – a place he knows he can always go. Poor lad's still
got a lot of changes ahead.'

'I know,' I said, feeling that familiar rush of guilt I always
got when we got to this stage with a placement. 'Will,
thank you *so* much for all this. Thanks a mill, Will, in fact.
You've gone above and beyond here, and we really appreciate it.'

'Not at all, Casey. All in the job, this kind of thing.'

Which I knew it probably was, but that didn't make me
appreciate him any less. He'd never been less than brilliant,
not to mention kind and enthusiastic, and – oh, I didn't
know – just so *up* for it himself. I was so glad he was Tyler's
social worker.

'Oh, and there's something else,' he said. 'You might also
be impressed by another piece of progress I think I've
made. Nothing set in stone yet, of course, but I think I just
might have found a placement for Tyler. Lovely couple.
They can't take him until after Christmas, so I thought
we'd hold off for a bit with any meetings, but still it's looking promising, so fingers crossed.'

I felt my heart lurch. Sort of leap into my mouth,
however physiologically impossible. There was a potential
placement for him already? It seemed he'd only been with

us for two minutes. Which was rubbish – it had been months now, and, of course, we always knew this day would come, but, oh, how I hated hearing those words.

I thanked Will as heartily as I could and hung up. Then I sat miserably for the next hour, as I always did at this point, writing up my latest notes in my foster-carer log, and after doing so I began flicking back through it. It was fat now – a wodge of fat files and notes and bits of paper, and I glanced through the notes of some of the other children we'd had living with us: Justin, Ashton and Olivia, who been with us for so long; Cameron – just a few days; Spencer – a few months; Sophia, little Abbie … So many children, so many painful goodbyes.

It was a form of masochism; turning the pages was like being struck repeatedly by a mallet, and before long there were tears rolling down my face. *Bloody fostering!* I thought. *What on earth had possessed me to do such a thing!*

Truth be told, I knew the answer. I did it because I loved it. This was just the cost we paid for all the joy. I needed to man-up and I did, as I'd done many times before, those gloomy thoughts being dusted away as carefully as the cobwebs in my conservatory, so that by the time Tyler and I set off on our journey to see aunt Angela I had my equilibrium and my smile back in place.

'I wonder if she looks like my mum,' Tyler called from the back seat of the car as we approached the estate on which she lived. 'I bet she does. I can't remember what Mum really looks like but the social lady said she'd seen a picture of her once and that she was very beautiful. She told me that.'

I smiled through the mirror. 'Well, I don't know if your auntie looks like her, sweetie – we shall have to see. But if your mum looked like you, then she will indeed have been very beautiful.'

He laughed at that. 'I can't be beautiful. I'm a *boy*, Casey – derr! Oh, but I'm dead nervous. If she asks me about where I live, or about my dad, or that witch, I'm gonna tell her I'm a foster kid because I don't want to live at home. If she finds out they don't want me, it might make her think I'm no good, mightn't it?'

'She will not,' I said firmly, 'and if she did, she'd be wrong. Couldn't be more wrong,' I added, for good measure.

So, I thought, Tyler had simply accepted then that he wasn't going home. No one had ever told him that. He'd just taken it as a given that they didn't want him. I hoped he wasn't back on his tack of being unwanted because he was unlovable. I watched him through the rear-view mirror. He couldn't be more lovable, in my book.

It was another 20 minutes before we pulled up outside what my sat nav called 'my destination', though as a destination address it wouldn't make *Homes & Gardens*. It was a bleak-looking, run-down semi on an equally bleak street of run-down semis, and having been doing this job for years now and the one I'd done before it, I had seen enough to know that the person who was waiting behind the front door would be one just clinging on to their independence.

'Looks like we're here,' I said, painting a smile on my face. Now we'd arrived I wondered if this had been a good idea after all. 'Look at you,' I said, going into bustle mode, 'you've got chocolate all around your mouth. Come here.' Tyler leaned towards me as I did that mumsy (and perhaps unforgivable) thing of taking out a tissue, dampening it on my tongue and then scrubbing the corners of his lips with it. He duly grimaced, but in a good-natured way. Then he grinned at me instead. 'Will I do now?'

'You'll do for me, kiddo,' I said as I let him out of the back. Then, for the first time that I could remember, he reached for my hand. I hadn't proffered it – he had just found it and grabbed it.

We were greeted at the door by a woman I knew was in her forties but who looked – understandably – much older. She was thin and gaunt, and though she had long sleeves covering her arms I couldn't help but wonder how many scars lay beneath.

'Hi there,' I said, smiling. 'You must be Angela. I'm Casey, and this is Tyler.'

Tyler smiled shyly at his aunt, still holding tight to my hand, but was almost knocked off his feet as she lunged forward for a hug.

'Hello there, little guy,' she said, smiling to reveal not so much a row of teeth as a row of gaps with the odd tooth still present. 'Oh my God,' she declared, 'you don't half look like your mummy!' She then let him go and stepped back into her hall. 'Come on then, come in, I've got the kettle on. Excuse the mess and the dog hairs, they're a bugger to get off the carpet.'

There was no sign of any actual dogs, but I assumed she'd locked them up somewhere. Out the back, perhaps, because there didn't seem to be another downstairs room. Just a through-lounge and a kitchen, the door to which was open, revealing a cluttered worktop and a clothes drying rack, slung with washing.

Tyler kept my hand in a vice-like grip as we followed her into the house. She led us into the through-lounge and pointed to her sofa. 'Make yourselves comfy,' she ordered. 'I'll just go get the teas. I got the lad some milk. That okay?'

Tyler nodded as she left the room. 'Casey,' he whispered, 'she looks a bit funny, don't you think?'

I stifled a smile. 'Tyler! You mustn't say that – it's rude. Just try to look beyond that. Try to get to know her a bit. She's probably as nervous as you are.'

I then tried to find a spot on the sofa that wasn't covered in dog hairs and God knew what else and, failing in both regards, sat down with Tyler gingerly. Angela *did* look kind of funny, I conceded, what with so many teeth gone. And her hair, obviously once black, was liberally streaked with grey and tied on the top of her head in a slightly skewed ponytail, so tightly that it seemed to pull at her face.

I tried my best to blank out the disorder that surrounded me (not to mention the sweetish, cloying, catch-in-the-throat smell) and graciously accepted the chipped mug of tea that she brought back, bearing the timeless legend *Have a Break, Have a Kit Kat*. It wasn't easy to drink. I didn't drink tea – I was a coffee person – and it wasn't helped by the greasy blobs floating on the surface. But not to drink it would have been ungracious so I sipped the scalding liquid as best I could, while Tyler, taking my lead, did the same with his beaker of milk.

Nowhere to Go

'How old's the lad?' Angela boomed, as she sat down on the adjacent armchair, slopping tea on the carpet as she lowered herself into the sagging seat.

'He's 12 now, aren't you, Tyler?' He nodded his confirmation, still looking as transfixed by her as he'd been when we'd first seen her. 'We're, er, off to the crematorium,' I went on, when she didn't answer. For all her decibel level, she seemed as awkward as we felt. And it suddenly hit me that her booming voice might be the result of her being deaf. Used to needing people to speak up – didn't that unconsciously make you raise your voice? I didn't know, but it seemed the most likely explanation. 'There's a memorial cross there,' I added. 'We thought we'd take some flowers, didn't we, Tyler? But the reason we wanted to come and meet you was because Tyler obviously doesn't remember his mum, and we thought you might be able to tell us a bit about her – whether you had any nice memories you could share with us … a few photographs, perhaps. Tyler hasn't got any,' I finished. 'Not one.'

Angela sighed and put her mug down on the carpet, where it slopped over again, the liquid joining the marbling of beige-y stains there. 'Look,' she said, frowning and slapping away some stray strands of escaped hair, 'I don't want you to think I'm being awkward or anything – and I did wanna see you, kid, honest – but, well, truth be told, I don't have much I *can* tell you. Truth is, lad, I was out of it most of the time,' she said, looking straight at Tyler. 'I was in a bad place back then – when our Fi was a youngster. And I never got my head straight, not before she died, at any rate. I was a crap sister, basically,' she added, shaking her head and looking genuinely regretful. 'I should have been look-ing out for her and I didn't. My problem – you know, the heroin and that – always came first. Before her, before my own kids –'

'Oh, you have children?' I said, my excitement at hear-ing this causing me to jump in before properly engaging my brain. Of course she didn't.

'Not no more,' she said, as if discussing a used car rather than flesh and blood. 'Got taken off me, both of 'em, soon as they were born. Not that I cared,' she added. 'Not a bit of it. I was that bad. Don't you touch drugs, son, you hear? Never.'

Touching though her words were, there was no sadness there, however – not for the children she'd never know. The children were probably adults now and would never know her either. Just the objective regret of a life not well lived. As a one-woman drug awareness and prevention programme for Tyler, she couldn't have been bettered. Her honesty was as refreshing as her surroundings smelled stale.

'So you see, kid,' she went on, 'I'm not a lot of use to you. As bad as it sounds –' She tapped her temple. 'My pigging brain is messed up, isn't it? I don't even have any memories of my own, so I don't have anything up there to give you. And I've only got one photo, so I can't let you have that. Sorry, but I can't. It's all I got to remember. I got to look at it, you see, so I can.'

Tyler nodded his understanding, and I wondered if he was taking all this in. He certainly didn't look angry or sad – just resigned. It was no more and no less than perhaps he expected. It was perhaps me who had hoped for a little more.

But I fixed on the positive. 'The photograph you have. Could we take a look?'

Angela turned to me, looking puzzled, as though she had already forgotten. 'Photograph?' she asked. Perhaps she had.

I nodded. 'Yes. You said you had one photo of your sister? Of Fiona? Can we look at it? I'm sure Tyler would like to see it.'

She stood up, and pulled the hoodie down, yanking it hard by either side. It felt so incongruous to see a woman of her age dressed the way she was. Incongruous, but what else should I have expected her to be wearing? Smart separates? Elegant footwear? She clearly only dressed to keep out the cold. 'You can look at it,' she said over her shoulder as she shuffled off to the back half of the room, 'but I can't let you take it. I'm sorry, kid, but it's all I have left.'

'That's okay,' Tyler said – the first thing he'd said in ages. 'I can take a photo *of* it. I have a smartphone.'

'A what phone?' she said, looking back towards us while rummaging in a drawer in a pine dresser.

'A smartphone,' Tyler said again. 'A BlackBerry.'

'Oh, one of those,' she said, heading back. 'You've got one that takes photos, have you? I know about those. Never likely to have one, though. Some of us can't afford such luxuries.' But she said it in a way that was not at all provocative and accompanied by what was probably a wink, directed at me. In another universe she'd make a great aunt

– even a kind of gran figure. But not this one. Which felt very sad.

Tyler held his phone up. 'It was a present,' he said. 'I got it for my birthday.'

'Ah, yes,' she said. 'I remember. You said you were 12. I thought it must have been recent, way you puffed up when you said it. Anyway, here you go. That's your mum.'

I moved closer to Tyler as he took it from her, so I could get a better look myself. The photo was old and curled and, strictly speaking, it was only half a photo. It had been ripped down the middle – in an effort, I presumed, to remove some undesirable.

'That weren't your dad,' Angela said, presumably reading our thoughts as she sat back down again. 'This was before that, and he was just some other shitty boyfriend she once had. Didn't want to have to look at his ugly face, either.'

Not that you would, I thought. No, your eye would immediately be drawn to her. Because, just like Tyler, she had the sort of eyes that just pulled you in. And it was funny, having seen so much of Tyler in his father, to see someone who looked even more like our young charge; same petite form, same indefinable *something* – I didn't know what it was, quite, but I hoped he could see it too.

She was dressed for the times, all early-nineties grunge-style, heavy eye make-up, pale face and hefty, mannish boots. She looked around 17, full of attitude, and reminded me of how Riley – just a little bit younger then – had gone on and on and on about N-Trance and Baby D, and how obsessed she'd been with having her hair permed. Not to mention how cross she'd been that I wouldn't let her.

'Go on, then,' I told Tyler, 'get your phone on the case. And take a few – maybe do a couple by the window with the flash off as well.'

I knew then, I think, that we wouldn't be coming back. There was nothing for Tyler here, and he knew it. I think Angela did too, as we said slightly stiff goodbyes and she told us half-heartedly to keep in touch. There was no spark of kinship – the drugs had put paid to that – and no sense of unfinished business either.

But we had our photo, and as we pulled out into the road to drive away Tyler pulled it up and gazed at his collection of images, looking at the face of the girl who'd chosen drugs over him, and I don't think he held it against her.

'That social worker lady was right, wasn't she?' I said softly. 'She was beautiful, love, wasn't she? And so like you, too. That really took my breath away, that did.'

He nodded. And then, out of the blue, he laughed out loud.

'What's funny?' I said, surprised. It was the last thing I'd been expecting.

'Weren't you terrified?' he asked. 'God, when she went to get that photo? Honest, Casey, I was thinking she'd look just like that lady did. That would have been just *awful*, wouldn't it?' He grinned at me then. 'So I was, like, *majorly*, like, *phew*!'

We'd had bad days and worse days and absolutely appalling days. But today, I thought, as I tucked Tyler into bed that night, had been unequivocally, gloriously good. Which was not to say, I decided, looking at the glow from his new screensaver, that it wouldn't provoke a weepy moment looking back.

'We'll get a print made from that,' I told him, nodding towards the photo on the screen once I'd kissed his cheek, said night, night and hoped the bed bugs wouldn't bite. 'Then you can have it framed and keep it by your bed.'

'That would be epic,' he said sleepily, turning onto his side. 'And Casey,' he added, turning back towards me again. 'I know you're *not* my mum, but …'

He fell silent again, clearly undecided about whether to say what he wanted to say.

'But what, love?' I coaxed softly. 'Go on. You can tell me.'

'I love you like you *were* my mum. That's all.'

Chapter 20

Winter seemed to arrive all at once. Only a few days after we'd been on our visit to see Angela the temperature plummeted enough to turn all the remaining greenery in my garden to whiskery, rigid silver statues.

'Do you want a lift to school this morning?' I asked Tyler, eyeing the view from the kitchen window and imagining how chilly it would be outside.

'I'm not a wuss, Casey,' he said, laughing. 'All my mates would take the mick out of me if I didn't turn up to meet them cos it was cold!'

He shook his head at me as though I were quite, quite mad and, shrugging off my suggestion of a scarf, grabbed his coat and was away, presumably before I could find him a bobble hat.

The house felt cold too – as if caught by surprise, and not quite yet able to cope. So I took my toast into the living room and ate it in front of the TV so I could take advantage of the heat from the fire.

I glanced up at the fireplace as I switched on the heat, at the latest addition to my collection of family photos. It was the photo of Tyler's mum, which I'd had him email me so I could download it to my laptop, in order that I could print off some physical copies. I'd then got a couple of frames, as I'd promised – one for his bedroom and one for here – and I knew it mattered to him greatly that I'd popped one alongside the kids and the grandkids. 'It's like she's part of the family, too, isn't it?' he'd observed happily.

I'd also printed a third copy, for Tyler's memory box. Almost all kids in care are encouraged to create memory boxes, and though it had been done in fits and starts – what with everything that had happened – Tyler's was very much a work in progress.

A memory box is exactly what you'd expect it to be. Usually a robust shoe or boot box, covered in shiny paper and personalised, it was a place to store family photographs, any certificates or awards the child might have won, school achievements, family anecdotes (not to mention foster-family anecdotes, where applicable), letters and postcards, ticket stubs from shows, cinema stubs and so on. Pretty much anything, really, that serves as a reminder of something important in their lives.

As Tyler had only just come back into the system, he didn't have one when he'd arrived with us, but Will had been helping him to address this lack, particularly as he would soon be moving on. This had been a watershed time for him, obviously, one marked with a degree of hurt and trauma, and it was important he had some good things to remember it by. Bits and bobs that would remind him of some fun times we'd had, to which end, whenever something struck me, or there was a photo that seemed apt, I'd print and/or pass it over to add to the box.

I continued to look at the picture as I sat back down with my toast. There was no doubt about it – Tyler's mother had been a beautiful young woman and, in this picture anyway, bore no physical evidence of the drug-addled addict she was so soon and so tragically to become. What was her past? What was her story? I wished I knew. I was also struck, as I'd been quite a bit these past weeks, by a niggling anxiety – quite unlike me – which I couldn't seem to shift, and whose source I couldn't seem to put my finger on.

Was it some mad menopausal hormonal upheaval? Just a reaction to the stress of fostering again? A belated response to the anxiety surrounding Riley's pregnancy after her previous miscarriage? Who knew? All I knew was that I was slightly out of kilter and couldn't work out why.

You're probably just getting stressed, Casey, I told myself sternly. *It's coming up to that mad Christmas rush time, after all.*

But that was the funny thing. Normally by now I'd been in full-on Christmas excitement mode, but this year I hadn't even really thought about it. Well, apart from telling Tyler we'd do a spot of Christmas shopping when we went to the cemetery – but that was nothing. I'd usually have half my presents wrapped by now.

My toast finished, I stood up, mentally shaking myself out of my funny mood. The truth was that I was also anxious about the cemetery trip. Despite Tyler assuring me it would be fine because he'd 'done graveyards now', I knew it would be emotionally charged for us both. And with it looming now – we were due to be driving there that weekend – I knew the best thing I could do right now was go and visit my daughter. There was no tonic better than being immersed in chit-chat and baby-talk, after all.

Levi and Jackson were both at school, of course, but when I arrived at Riley's a couple of hours later Marley Mae was definitely making her presence known. Almost seven months old now, she'd found her preferred method of getting around, which consisted of a strange mixture of crawling, rolling and a sort of 'bum shuffle'. It was as entertaining to watch as it was complicated to do and it struck me how much my grand-daughter reminded me of my daughter, who'd always gone her own way as well. Marley Mae had also found her voice, which was less agreeable at times, admittedly – a high-pitched scream followed by an indecipherable babble, which greeted me now, as I made my entrance.

'Oh look, it's Nanny,' Riley cried, 'and are we glad to see her!'

She bent down to pick up various bricks, blocks and toy cars so that I could step into the room unobstructed. She was still in pyjamas and I suspected David had probably done the school run. Bless her – it was a tiring time of life. 'Come on in, Mum,' she said, 'and, seriously, I am *so* glad to see you. She's been a right handful today.'

'Today? It's only 11 o'clock!'

'Yes, and my day started at 5, Mum! God, she so should have been a boy, this kid.'

I laughed as I watched my grand-daughter follow her mummy round the room. Riley was right; that there was not a doll or pram or anything pink in sight wasn't quite the point, no – she had older brothers, so was living in a house full of boy-toys. But something told me she wouldn't become a girly-girl anyway; she was a tough little thing with a fondness for rough and tumble, and I suspected she might stay that way too.

'Go on,' I said to Riley. 'You go and have a soak in the bath – and take as long as you want, love. I'll deal with all this and with madam here for a bit.'

'You know what?' she said. 'If Justin Timberlake himself walked in right now, offering to whisk me off and ravish me, I think I'd turn him down for that, Mum.'

I knew exactly what she meant.

An hour or so later, with the little madam worn out and snoozing on a blanket in her play pen, Riley and I chatted over bacon sandwiches in the kitchen.

'So,' Riley said, 'what's going on in *your* life? I feel I've been a bit out of the loop the last few days. How's Tyler doing now?'

I filled her in – telling her about the auntie and the upcoming cemetery visit and, being the astute girl that she was, she frowned at me.

'And?' she said.

'And what?'

'And what's on your mind, Mum? Is there something else? Something you're not telling me?'

I laughed. 'What are you like?' I said. 'No, no, nothing at all, honest. I think I'm just a bit angsty about our visit at the weekend, that's all.'

'Hmm,' Riley said, looking at me suspiciously. 'Really? It's not like you to fret over something like that. I think you're hiding something from me.'

'Don't be daft, you silly sod. Hiding something? Why would I hide something from you?'

Even so, even *she* had noticed that I wasn't quite myself. Weird, I thought. Because she was right, it wasn't like me. And as we talked – mostly about the new bathroom suite David was putting in – I only half-listened, really, now somewhat fixated on my odd mood. The mood for which I had no explanation or answers. Perhaps I was sickening for something. Was that it?

I didn't seem to be; not if the rest of the week was anything to go by, it passing via the usual round of grandkids (Mike and I took Tyler and Jackson swimming while Levi was at a party), of kids (Kieron and Mike took Tyler to football, which meant a machine load of disgusting kit to deal with), of parents (I took Mum and Dad to the supermarket to get some groceries) and paperwork, none of which sent me into a state of malaise.

All in all, it was a drama-free, nice, happy week, so by the time Saturday came around I had to conclude that I was not ill, merely slightly askew. But there was a job to do, and Tyler and I were off to do it.

'One other job first, though,' I told Tyler as we parked in the big city-centre shopping mall we'd be visiting again later. 'Operation Billy Bear the second.'

He giggled as I pulled my purse from my handbag. 'Right, young man,' I said, pulling out a crisp ten-pound note. 'Your mission, should you choose to accept it, is to find a small blue fluffy thing that resembles Billy Bear the First. You must also find some flowers, and we have half an hour in which to complete. Should you fail to comply or complete the mission, however, that money will, of course, self-destruct.'

'Let me guess,' Tyler said as he listened increasingly incredulously, 'that's something cool from the olden days, right?'

'Cheeky beggar,' I chastised playfully. 'It's actually from *Mission Impossible*. You know about *Mission Impossible*, don't you? Tom Cruise? Though you're right, it is from the olden days – originally, that is. It's … Oh never mind. Come on, we don't have long for this, do we?'

The flowers were no problem, there being a big stand close by, from which Tyler chose a colourful mix of lilies and chrysanthemums, to place at his mum's cross along with his letter. 'I'll let you read this when we get there,' he'd said as he'd patted his pocket on our way out of the front door. We still had a blue bear to find somewhere, however, and this understandably took a little longer, blue bears coming in many shapes and sizes. We finally settled on one that he deemed very similar. 'Though mine had a white T-shirt on, so it's not quite the same,' he said. 'D'you think my mum will mind?'

'Mind? No, she'll *love* it, sweetie. Trust me, she'll be thrilled,' I said, figuring that, with a lump already forming in my throat, it was a lost cause hoping to spend the day dry-eyed. But how could anyone? I reasoned as we got back on the road. Still, that was par for the course. This was an emotional day in Tyler's life – making contact with a mum about whom he knew so little.

I wasn't even sure how much he did know about his mother; what, if anything, social services had told him. He knew how he'd been found, of course, but what did he know of his mum's life before him? I knew almost nothing about any of it. Did he? Surely at some point he would have demanded answers from his dad. I decided to ask him.

'Love,' I said, 'we've never talked that much about your mum, have we? I know you were very young when she died, but has anyone ever talked to you about her?'

He looked thoughtful for a moment. 'What, like my dad?'

'Yes, your dad. Or maybe your social worker – you know, when you first went to live there?'

'My dad never did, really. He was always, like, you don't want to know. But there was this lady who used to come – though I hardly remember her – and she was the one who said I was wet and starving when they found me. I don't remember any of that myself, though.'

'I know about that bit,' I said, nodding, 'and it's good you don't remember, don't you think? That would be such a horrible memory to have, wouldn't it? But did she tell you anything about your mum's life? Like if she had a job? Or the sort of things she liked? Liked doing?'

'No. I don't think she worked,' he said. 'She was on drugs, so she couldn't. I used to tell Cam that, did you know? That if he turned into a druggie, he'd never be able to get a job, because he'd have to be taking drugs all the time. There was one thing, though, that the lady told me. She said I used to have a nan – well, a lady who would've been my nan if I'd been born yet. But she died of something – she was my mum's mum – and that woman Angela's too, I suppose. I think it was cancer. And she said that's why my mum became a druggie. Because she and her sister didn't have anyone to look after them any more.' He gazed out of the window for a bit, but was suddenly galvanised. 'Hey, Casey?' he asked, just as I was about to respond to what he'd said previously, 'd'you think that's why she ended up doing drugs, because that Angela made her do it? Cos she was like, *loads* older, wasn't she? And that's what happens, doesn't it? Like you and Mike saying to me I shouldn't hang out with older boys, really – even if they are friends, because they can lead you astray.'

Once again, I was struck by the way he'd thought it through. And, yes, I thought, it could well have happened just as he'd suggested. I wondered how old Fiona and Angela had been when their mum had died. What might have happened? Might they have been left in some council house somewhere, the older sister being charged to take care of the younger? If Fiona had been in her teens, that could well have happened – if 16, it was really quite likely.

I'd probably never be able to find the answers, and neither would Tyler, but perhaps it wouldn't help to know anyway – not really. And that feeling only intensified when he made his next utterance. 'You know something?' he said, as if having discovered a great wisdom. 'I know lots of dead people, don't I?'

I sighed then and nodded. 'It seems that way, love, doesn't it? Let's hope that from now on it stops, eh? Let's hope that wherever you end up, it's a happy, happy place. One where you don't have to see any more drugs and sadness.'

And I felt so sad, even as I said it.

We arrived at our second cemetery in roughly as many weeks and it occurred to me how similar these places always seemed to be. The long drive through a pretty landscape, the presence of water ... only this time it was a small lake, rather than a stream. Then, at the end of the drive, the cemetery building – in this case a crematorium with a chapel adjacent, both buildings whitewashed and well bedded into their surroundings.

I took Tyler's hand as we walked from the car to the reception, where a man in a grey suit introduced himself as a Mr James, and explained that Tyler's mum's death had been recorded in the book of remembrance, which he then showed to Tyler. It was just a line – a simple entry that recorded her death and the date of her cremation.

'I understand that there's some kind of memorial here for Fiona,' I said, aware just how unimpressed Tyler seemed to be, to have come all this way for a line in a book.

'That's right,' the funeral director said. 'There's a cross in the garden of remembrance. But there's something more.' He looked down at Tyler with a kindly smile. 'There's also a plaque.'

'What's a plaque?' Tyler asked.

'Like a sort of brick,' Mr James said, 'that people pay to have displayed here, on a lease. Made of granite, and inscribed with your mother's name. You'll find it in the main hall. Shall I take you there first?'

This was a surprise. I'd done my research about council burials and cremations, and this was something I hadn't figured on at all.

'There it is,' Mr James said, pointing just above head height to one of many similar plaques that filled the wall. 'There's your mum's memorial, young man.'

I gasped as I read it, truly gobsmacked.

My beautiful sister, Fiona Lessing, Forever young.

Beneath it was her date of birth and her date of death. Such simple words, yet so revealing. And from Angela! Well, unless she had another sibling or half-sibling, and I was pretty certain that she didn't. Would have put money on it, in fact. I turned to Tyler. His chin was wobbling, so I put an arm round him and pulled him close. 'Well, I never,' I whispered. 'I wasn't expecting that! Were you?'

'She never said,' Tyler sniffed. 'Why'd she never say about that?'

'Who knows?' I said. 'Perhaps she knew she didn't need to.'

'Or p'raps she just forgot,' he answered sagely.

* * *

Mr James then took us outside, leading us to a large, very beautiful enclosed garden, enclosed by an almost unbroken square of memorial benches, where he told us we could stay as long as we liked, and also asked us if we could place any offerings not by the crosses themselves but on the benches and in the urns left for the purpose at the garden's borders.

It was an emotional place to be, reminding me of those fields you'd see pictures of in northern France and Belgium, where crosses marked fallen soldiers for as far as the eye could see. The scale was obviously smaller here, but it was arresting and moving even so.

Mr James left us at the row where Fiona's cross was located and within a few steps we were standing in front of it. Gazing down at it was unexpectedly moving.

'Sweetie,' I said gently, 'I'm just going to leave you alone for a minute. I'll put these flowers and the bear over on that bench for you, if that's okay.'

Tyler turned and looked up at me, his eyes full of tears. 'But what about my letter, Casey? I wanted to leave my letter on her cross. If we leave it over there it might blow away.'

I thought for a moment. Mr James hadn't actually said anything about letters, but no other cross had anything attached to it that I could see, and I didn't know what best to suggest. Then I had a moment of possibly divine inspiration. 'You know what?' I said. 'Rather than just leave the letter, Tyler, why don't you read it out to your mum instead? I think that's better anyway, because that way she'll hear your voice reading it to her, won't she? It'll be like hearing your thoughts out loud, wouldn't it?'

He seemed to like that idea, and pulled the letter from his pocket, holding it tightly so it didn't blow away.

I felt the need to leave him then, and walked the few steps back to the end of the row, but in the silence I could hear him speaking anyway.

Dear Mum

I'm sorry you had to die when I was so little and I wish I could have known you. I'm not mad at you any more and I know you were sad. I'll try to be a good lad so's you can be proud of me. I didn't like the mum I got after you. She was horrible to me. But I've got Casey, and she's epic, and so's Mike. But I got to move again because I'm in fostering, so I'm going to be getting a new mum after Christmas, but I'll write again and tell you what she's like.

PS Can you please look after my best friend, Cameron? He's got browny blond hair and he's funny, but he's dead now.

All my love for ever, your son, Tyler

By the time Tyler had refolded the letter I was in pieces. As was he, so I rushed back down the row and pulled him into my arms. I didn't know what to say, but that was fine. There was nothing to be said. In fact, it was Tyler who broke the silence, with another belated PS.

'Bye, Mum,' he said, stroking the cross as we prepared to leave it. 'Now I know when your birthday is, I'll come back to see you.' He then looked at me. 'We can, can't we, Casey?'

I nodded without thinking, before it really hit me that it probably wouldn't be me who brought him back to this place. His mother's birthday wasn't until June.

Chapter 21

I remember when my gran died. I remember I was inconsolable. I remember coming back from her funeral and climbing into bed and not wanting to come out again, ever. I'd been 13 and I remember how well-meaning grown-ups had kept telling me that 'life goes on' and how ridiculous a thing it seemed to me to say. My beloved gran hadn't gone on, had she? And I didn't want to. Just wanted it to stop and let me be till I felt better.

So when we returned home from our trip and Tyler said he wanted to go to bed, I was more than happy to let him and to leave him for as long as he needed. He was exhausted – both mentally and, as a consequence, also physically. It's so easy to forget how the act of crying can be so debilitating; how it drains you, how it makes your eyes sting and your throat sore and your chest ache. And he had cried. He had cried buckets. He was drowning in his tears now. Tears he'd needed to shed, but which had taken their toll.

* * *

Tyler slept through on Saturday, and though he came down for breakfast on Sunday morning he went back upstairs and slept most of Sunday away too. Indeed, by Sunday evening I was beginning to think that he'd need to stay off school on Monday as well. But he didn't. On Monday morning he came down and, though he was still a bit quiet, I could tell he was on the road to recovery by the fact that he'd already sniffed out the batch of chocolate brownies I'd made and wanted to know if he could have one in his lunchbox.

'Unless they're for something else,' he said. 'Some family thing you've got happening today or something.'

'Tyler,' I said, laughing, 'do you *really* think I'd make a batch of chocolate brownies and leave you out? That would be almost like a criminal offence!'

I pulled the lid off his box to show him that there were already two nestling in there. 'See?' I said, giving him a playful nudge. 'You're as daft as a brush, you.'

'Yeah, but they *might* have been. I didn't want to just make presumpshions.'

I told him he could preshump all he liked but right now it was time he left for school, and after he'd donned coat and gloves and conceded to a scarf at last I stood on the doorstep and thought about his words, waving till he'd crossed the road and turned the corner.

Yes, he was definitely on the mend. He just seemed so much lighter of heart, somehow. It wasn't something readily noticeable – not by any old anyone, anyway – but by me it was, because I knew him so well.

Still, his words left a mark that stayed right through my making coffee, and right till I was halfway down my second mug. 'Some family thing,' he'd said. He'd wondered if they'd been earmarked for 'some family thing', as if that wouldn't include him – *didn't* include him, despite us spending so many months telling him the opposite, that we were his foster carers and that while we had him he was very much one of our family. Not a guest, not a visitor. Just one of us.

I drained my second coffee, aware of something else as well. That, for some inexplicable reason, I felt like crying. What the hell was wrong with me? Yes, I knew I always felt a bit like crying at this point, but this was different. I really did want to just sit and blub. And then I started thinking about Will, and the conversations he'd likely be having with Tyler now, preparing him for whatever he'd been preparing for him after Christmas – a meeting with his new foster family perhaps? I didn't know. The last couple of times we'd spoken I'd been too chicken to ask. Was it Will's influence that had Tyler talking of 'some family thing' that by definition didn't include him? Was that a part of the preparation as well?

'I don't want him to go,' I told my mum that lunchtime, round at her and Dad's house. 'I really, really don't want him to go, Mum.'

She paused in the beating she was doing – she was making omelettes for lunch and had thrown in some extra eggs for me. 'And this is *news*?'

'What d'you mean?' I asked, struck by her odd reaction. At the very least I'd been expecting 'There there's. 'Yes, it *is* news,' I added. 'I'm dreading it, Mum, honestly. And, yes,

I know what you're going to say, and you're right. I *do* always dread it. But I'm dreading it so much *more* this time, for some reason. That's what I wanted to ask you. You started the menopause around my age, didn't you? Is this hormonal, feeling like this? Feeling so tearful and wet-raggy and generally pathetic? You think that might be it? That I've started the menopause?'

Mum shook her head and went back to her beating for a few seconds. 'Sweetheart,' she said finally, 'that's not it. Well,' she added, 'not as far as I can see, anyway. Yes, you might be starting but I don't think it's that, and nor does Riley …'

'Riley? What's Riley got to do with this? Have you been talking?'

She grinned. 'Is that illegal then? Me talking to my grand-daughter?'

'No, of course it's not. But if you've been talking about *me*, spill the beans, please.'

'Casey, love, you know exactly what the problem is – we've both said it, and your dad agrees. You've fallen in love with this kid and that's all there is to it.'

'Mum, I fall in love with all of them – that's a given.'

But she was already shaking her head. 'I know,' she said, 'but not the way you've fallen in love with this one. Well, this one and our Justin – be honest, if you hadn't just started out fostering you'd have kept Justin too. Don't deny it.'

I stared at her open-mouthed. 'Er, pardon? Kept Justin *too*? What are you on about?'

'You want to keep Tyler, love. So I don't know why you don't just see if you *can* keep him. Well, speak to Mike about it first, obviously, but as I was saying to your dad yesterday, for what possible reason would you let him go?'

She stopped beating the eggs then and put a pan on the hob ready. 'Love, admit it – this time it's different. He wants to be *your* kid, not farmed off to another lot of strangers. And you want to be his mum. It's that simple. And –' she said, raising a finger to stop me from interrupting, 'if you let him go you will regret it. I *know* you will. And you do too, so stop all this "being in denial" nonsense, or whatever Riley calls it. Menopause, my eye,' she finished, grinning at me again.

And she was right to point it out. Right to try and persuade me to stop denying it. I knew it was the answer – I'd just been too scared to ask the question. Too scared to pull it up from the place deep inside me where I could safely bury it so it couldn't surge up to hurt me. She'd been right about Justin too, but that had been different. Back then it was never going to be an option. But now? What *was* stopping me, exactly? A zillion things, actually. Logistical things, practical things, emotional things, others' needs.

'Mum, it's not as simple as that,' I began.

'Fiddlesticks. Of course it is! Casey,' she said, looking at me sternly and waggling her non-stick fish slice. 'If that kid has a chance of a happy life with you, and it's within your power to provide it, then you should ring that John and ask him. Bugger the protocol, just *ask* him, for goodness' sake. And do it quickly before they find someone else.'

I felt like crying again then, remembering what he'd said to me after Cameron's funeral about loving me like I was his mother, and what he'd said in his letter to his real mum, that being with us was epic. But that didn't necessarily make it possible. 'Mum,' I said, 'you're wrong, it really *isn't* that simple. They've already found a couple, wheels have been put in motion, and, anyway, it's not what we signed up for. We're supposed to be delivering these specialist –'

'And bugger what you signed up for, as well!' my mum said with feeling. 'Specialist programmes or otherwise! And if it's about rules, what about when they send you kids who aren't right for the programme? That's okay, isn't it? They can put it to one side, then, when it suits them, can't they? And they do. So now, just for a change, tell them that this is what suits *you*. Casey, you won't know unless you ask them, will you?'

My father shuffled in then, looking from one of us to the other. 'Food isn't going to be happening any time soon then, I take it?' he asked. 'Because all I can hear is you two yakking!'

And though it's an expression that's over-used, I could have used it at that moment. I really *didn't* know whether to laugh or cry.

Once the idea took root, there was no stopping it. What exactly was standing between me and this thing mushrooming inside me – this thing that I knew was the right thing for me, and hopefully for Mike, and without a doubt the right thing for Tyler? A lot of things, basically, I thought as I drove home again, fuelled by a mixture of petrol and cheese omelette and sheer excitement. So I would have to go through them – possibly draw up a list of pros and cons, perhaps, and once I'd done that (and I didn't have long till Tyler came home from school now, either) I would have to consider how best to approach both the small hurdle that was John, and the rather larger hurdle that was Mike.

But I was optimistic. Another half hour in Mum and Dad's company and I could already see that, actually, it could work. Tyler had done the programme, and that meant a great deal in itself, because though there would doubtless be all sorts of challenges to come, he had at least proved that he was malleable and sufficiently biddable for us to maintain parental control. And with that proven (well, as far as it was capable of being proven) I would still be free, I reckoned, to continue to foster; take new children in and put them on the programme, just as I'd done before.

But Mike – how would he feel about this kind of arrangement? I didn't know. And that was a shock in itself; that, for perhaps the first time in three decades together, I had absolutely no idea how my husband would react to this bombshell. And bombshell it would certainly be. It was one thing knowing how to sweet talk him into taking a new placement on after saying we'd have a sabbatical, but quite another to say, *Oh, by the way, let's hang on to this latest child for another six or seven years*. No, I'd have to choose my moment and my words very carefully.

In the meantime, I decided, when I arrived home and went indoors I would at least get the small hurdle out of the way.

And John turned out to be a somewhat larger hummock. Not negative – he could hardly think us unsuitable, after all, but not quite as 'Sure, it shall be so' as I'd perhaps anticipated.

For starters, he was shocked, so he clearly hadn't been talking to my mother. 'You sure about this?' were his first words. 'You've completely thrown me,' being his second. He then went on to explain that people like me and Mike were a scarce specialist resource and that there were implications to us taking on Tyler long term. 'You know how it works,' he said, even though I hardly needed it explaining. 'One of the criteria in taking on kids such as you and Mike do is that it's one on one – that you don't get asked to take it on if you have other children in the family home. Particularly kids who have troubles themselves.'

'Yes, I know that,' I said, 'but it struck me that there's an argument to be made here. Having Tyler around could actually be of benefit, couldn't it? To both kids. And it's not like we're not very experienced at this now …'

'Well, it can't hurt,' he conceded. 'There's no reason why we can't ask. Leave it with me. I'll sit down and have a word with the powers that be, and speak to Will too, of course – assuming you haven't already done that? He's the one who really has the final say in where Tyler goes, after all. But I can't promise,' he finished, deflating me somewhat. 'These things are never as cut and dried as you might think.'

'Aye, aye, Captain,' I said, smiling to myself, even so. If they weren't cut and dried than I would cut them up and dry them up personally. 'And thank you *so* much, John,' I gushed at him. 'And I promise you, if it comes off, we're not going to stop the fostering. I know we can make this work, I really do.'

'Well, we'll see,' said John, not sounding quite as convinced as he might have done. But I'd never been surer of anything.

Chapter 22

I just had time to call Riley before Tyler was due home and to tick her off for conniving with her grandmother.

'Hardly conniving,' she corrected. 'Just making astute observations. Aww, I wish I'd had money on it now.'

'You cheeky mare,' I said. 'Anyway, as recompense, I need a favour. I need to speak to your father about a certain young man and I obviously need the young man not to be around.'

'Bring him round to ours for tea,' she offered immediately. 'Oh and you might want to dig a tin hat out from somewhere. I've a feeling Dad might not be so gung ho as you are, so you might have some brickbats to dodge.'

'Oh don't say that, love. He loves Tyler, I know he does,' I felt duty bound to point out.

'I'm only kidding you,' she reassured me. 'For what it's worth, I think you're right, so you never know, do you? Well, if you pitch it right, that is.'

I laughed. 'Have you heard of Babe Ruth, daughter dear?'

'Nope,' she replied.

'Then go and Google it,' I laughed, hanging up.

'Good God in heaven, Casey!' Mike exclaimed as he took in the scene in front of him. 'What on earth have you done?'

He cast his eyes around then, past the steaks nestling on their bed of courgettes and peppers, past the mushroom and blue cheese topping, past the sides of sweetcorn and onion rings, and even past the fat, triple-cooked chips.

He looked up, down and all around, in fact, as if to find evidence of disaster, before returning his steady gaze to me.

'You old cynic,' I ticked him off, pouring him a glass of red wine. 'Can't I spoil you without you immediately jumping to the conclusion that I have some sort of scurrilous ulterior motive?'

'Nope,' he said, picking up a chip and popping it in his mouth.

'Well, I haven't,' I said. 'I just thought that since Tyler's out to tea, you and I could enjoy a little "us" time.'

And as soon as I said it, I could have kicked myself. Hardly the best time to bring the notion of 'us' time into the equation, after all – not when I was about to crush all hopes of 'us' time for the foreseeable future.

'Liar,' he said brightly, pulling out his chair and picking up his cutlery. 'Casey, trust me, I know you well enough by now. You've either been at the credit card for some unnecessary purchase, or you've booked some extravagant holiday, or you're about to ask me something that you think I'll say no to. Now spill, woman. It's going to be one of them, after all, and you might as well spit it out and tell me which.'

'Honestly,' I huffed, joining him and trying to think where to start. In my experience, it was best to prepare the ground a little first before launching into the main – and, in this case, somewhat contestable – master plan. So I tried to make small talk, working through Riley and the little ones, to what was on television that evening, via the Christmas lights I was still waiting for him to string up outside the house.

Then, halfway through the meal, he sat back and burst out laughing. Just like that. No provocation, no warning, no nothing. Just a great big guffaw of a laugh.

'What?' I said. 'What did I say that was so funny?'

'It's not what you said, it's what you didn't say that was funny. Oh, Case, I can't keep it up any longer, love, I really can't. But, fair play, it was fun while it lasted, watching you work.'

'Mike!' I snapped, '*Please*. What the hell are you going on about?'

'I know,' he said simply. 'I know all about it. Your dad called me at work earlier, wanted to know if we had any pallets going begging. And was obviously off-message because he told me.'

'About Tyler?' I asked.

He nodded. 'Well, the business part, at any rate.' He laughed again. 'I could hear your mum ticking him off in the background as well. No steak for him tonight, eh?'

'And?' I said, crossing my fingers under the table.

'And I was wondering – have you run it past John yet?'

I nodded. 'Theoretically. But *only* theoretically, I promise. I mean, obviously, it's all down to you, love. I mean, if you're set against it, then we obviously –'

'Case,' he said, 'I'm not.'

'Really, Mike? Honestly? It's a big thing. Extremely big.'

'*Really*, love. *Honestly*. And you know what's really funny? As soon as your dad let slip it was as if you had arrived at a solution to a problem I didn't even know we had. Does that make sense?'

I got up and threw my arms around him. 'Oh, thank God, thank God, thank God. Honestly, I've been on pins, wondering how you'd react. I mean we were supposed to be having a break, and … oh, you are a sod, Mike – you should have phoned me.'

'You kidding? I might be soft, but I'm not soft in the head, Case.' He nodded towards his plate. 'Miss out on this? Now that *would* be soft in the head. I take it there's something nice for pudding too?'

Things happened very quickly after that. I called John again the next day and told him that Mike was on board and that after sleeping on it we still felt the same way. John insisted we thought longer – this was a very big commitment. We, more than most people, knew the implications for Tyler if we took him on and then later had a change of heart.

But we didn't need telling that because we did know the implications – had lived though those kinds of implications with other kids ourselves. No, we were sure – the only stumbling block was the interminable red tape involved; we'd be talking about a change in status – changing from short-term to long-term carers, but then again not – which meant jumping through various administrative hoops.

Will, in the meantime, once put in the picture, held fire on the family he'd been speaking to about Tyler who, being foster carers, were used to plans changing with children, and wanted nothing more than for him to be where he'd be happy. And in the midst of it all there was Tyler to whom we told absolutely nothing; Tyler who was busy steeling himself for the inevitable – that he wasn't going home and that he wasn't staying with us and that he'd be on the move again in the new year. It was so hard, that part – that not telling him complication. Because I've never felt quite so much like I might burst.

We heard about the first part – that we could keep Tyler – another week later. By now we were into December and I was beginning to worry that, with the wheels of bureaucracy being what they were, we might have to agonise till January. But not so.

'Everyone's happy for you to keep Tyler long term,' John announced in what was beginning to seem like an endless stream of phone calls since we'd all sat down to discuss the practical implications of what becoming long-term foster carers involved. 'Not that it was ever really an issue,' he added quickly, 'but it's finalised now, anyway – so you can go ahead and let Tyler know now, if you want to. I know you've been champing at the bit.'

There was still a bit to do about maintaining our short-term status, as it wasn't usual to be doing both at the same time. But again, John was confident that the panel would approve us, at which point we'd be able to take new kids as well, either to go on the programme, or for respite.

Which mattered, of course, because we wanted to continue, but I'd been surprised by just how pragmatic I felt. If it turned out we couldn't then so be it, we couldn't. We'd have Tyler. And that mattered more.

All that remained, then, was to share the news with the boy himself, which we decided to do at home, the whole family together – pressing home the point that this had been a whole family decision. That the whole family wanted him as part of our family and – though I didn't need to mention this to anyone at any point – that this would in fact be the last 'family thing' that was going to be arranged without him. He was family now. It was official. Well, as long as that was what *he* wanted.

When a child is soon to leave you, they tend to detach. The nature of short-term foster care of the kind we've always done and still do is to provide a bridge between the bad place and the child's future happiness; a crucial stop-gap to prepare them for the next part. So the detachment is necessary, and it happens in both obvious and subtle ways. Sometimes it's instinctive in a child – particularly if they've been 'in the system' for a while – because it's a defence mechanism to protect them from the pain of parting. In some extreme cases children don't attach much at all; they're too canny, too self-protective. And with others it's a process involving the adults looking after them – using things like the memory box, to put a timeline into perspective, and often involving a phased introduction (visits and then sleepovers) to the family who are taking the reins.

The next step with Tyler would have been to meet his next foster family, and as far as he knew that was what was going to happen. He didn't know when, but he wasn't stupid – Will had told him how things worked – and having made his wishes clear back in October (that he wanted us to be his mum and dad now) he'd retreated to the place he thought it was necessary for him to occupy; one of acceptance that it wasn't happening, that he was moving on.

And what a lot of water had flowed under that bridge. In the space of seven months Tyler's life had changed beyond recognition. He'd left the family home that had never really felt like a family, and with time and distance it seemed clear that this was by far the best thing for him – better to be with warm-hearted, committed strangers than in a home where you're really not wanted. The rapid turn-around in his behaviour seemed to be testament to that. So he'd adapted, reasonably well, only to have his brother reject him too, and to compound that he had to live through his friend's death.

But there was good news, as well – we had found him his mother, and who knew just how big a thing that would prove to be for him. It could be life changing, even. Better still, now there was no question of them having him back, his 'parents' had agreed that there *could* be some sibling contact; something both boys (now that Grant had stood firm *re* his brother) desired and would benefit from.

And now, as far as he knew, it would be Christmas at the Watsons, followed by whatever else life had in mind for him. And I couldn't wait to tell him what that was.

'We're having a party night,' I told him on the last day of school. I'd come to pick him up, something I didn't usually do. 'A big family party, at home,' I explained. 'Starting in half an hour. So chop, chop – we'd better get our skates on.'

'Is it someone's birthday?' he wanted to know as he did up his seat belt. 'Or is it an early one for Christmas? Or, Casey …' he said, clearly having had another thought, 'is it the one Will was saying about for my golden-sheet thingy?'

'None of those,' I said. 'Your award thing will be happening after Christmas, love. No,' I lied, 'this is just what we always do on the last day of term. Get everyone round so we can get into the Christmas spirit. That's why I had to pick you up,' I finished, 'because I didn't want you dawdling. We still have to get ready, don't we?'

'Oh, man,' he said, doing one of his little fist pumps. 'A party! This day just keeps getting better and better!'

You want better, you got better, I thought excitedly, as we drove home. It was almost impossible not to do a fist pump myself.

It was definitely impossible to maintain any sort of composure when we got there, knowing, even as Tyler dumped his bag and hung his coat up, that just on the other side of the living room door were Mike, Riley and David, Mum and Dad, Kieron and Lauren and – being brilliantly distracted from giving themselves away – Levi and Jackson and little Marley Mae.

'Shall I go up and change?' Tyler asked me, his eyes shining. 'Put my best clobber on? Or are there jobs we need to do?'

'Clobber? Now there's a word,' I said. 'And yes, there is one job. D'you think you could go into the living room for me and, er …' Nope, all of a sudden I couldn't seem to think of anything plausible. 'Go and …' Where was my brain when I needed it? Nothing. 'Just go into the living room,' I settled on, while he looked at me quizzically.

'Casey, have you gone all loopy?' he asked me, giggling.

'You know what?' I said, opening the door for him. 'I think I have.'

Perhaps appropriately, the first thing he saw was his teddy – the teddy Will had pulled out all the stops to retrieve for him. It had travelled from the old house along with every-thing else in that cupboard and it was really only a question of someone making an *effort* to find it. And, finally, Grant had done so and now Billy Bear the First was here.

'Wha—?' Tyler said, seemingly oblivious to everyone in there, his eyes going past all the familiar faces that he had expected to see anyway, to the bear, which he obviously hadn't. The blue bear, which was sitting atop a big blue cake, which was sitting at the centre of a table full of food, which was sitting through the arch, in the dining room. 'Is that him? Is that Billy Bear?' he asked me. '*Really?*'

'Indeed it is,' I said. 'Why don't you go and say hello to him? I expect he's missed you.'

'An' there's cake!' piped up Jackson. 'For you!'

'And it's not for your birthday,' added Levi. 'It's a *special* cake. And it's got words on. Writ specially for you.'

'What's it say then?' Tyler asked, as the three boys approached it.

'It says welc—' Jackson began.

'Shh!' said Riley. 'Let Tyler read it.'

Tyler read it. I watched him mouth each word, taking it all in.

'It says "Welcome to your new home!", Tyler,' Jackson persisted.

'He *knows* that,' his older brother said. 'He *can read*, you know!'

Tyler turned to us all then, staring as if seeing us properly for the first time. 'For ever?' he said, looking at me. 'For ever till I'm a grown-up?'

I could only nod, because by now I was way too choked up to speak.

'That's right, kiddo,' Mike answered for me. 'For ever till you're a grown-up. If you want, son, that is. What do you think?'

Tyler carefully took his bear from the cake and put it close to his ear.

Then he grinned and had Billy Bear the First do his fist pump for him.

'We both think that's *epic*,' he replied.

A note to the reader

I'll bet you didn't see that coming, did you? And you wouldn't be alone, because, back then, trust me, neither did I. So there was no unhappy ending to this particular story, you'll be pleased to know. No tearful parting. No wrenching of any heartstrings. No pain. Though I have to admit, I shed more tears over Tyler than I think I ever have, before or since.

Mike and I were invited to a special panel hearing, a couple of weeks into the new year, where we were formally re-assessed for approval. It went better than we had hoped: we were approved to foster one long-term child and up to two other children; either short term, on our programme, or, where required, just for respite. This was important. It meant that should we be needed to take in siblings we could take both rather than see them split up.

Tyler still lives with us (yes, I've kept him a secret up until now) and he continues to thrive. His brother, Grant, comes to visit regularly and we are now all very close – he's even joined us for a family holiday a couple of times.

Tyler's doing well at school, too. He works hard and, despite some teasing from his mates, is taking Childcare as a GCSE option; the only boy on the course. Who knows where it will take him? But neither Mike nor I would be surprised if he ended up working with kids, like our Kieron. And he's turning out to be like Kieron in another way, too. Another self-proclaimed girl-magnet (like we didn't see *that* coming …), who would rather stick pins in his eyes than go to school without his hair gel and ten minutes in the mirror!

As for Alicia and Gareth, it's been a case of acceptance. Though I'll never accept the way they treated Tyler – particularly Alicia – we've all come to terms with the sad but not uncommon reality that they only ever took him on reluctantly, at best, and that he never really did fit into their lives. As things stand, though, they still receive regular updates about his progress and everyone seems happy for this arrangement to carry on.

And it certainly seems to work for Tyler. 'I have two mums,' he tells people. 'One who's passed away, and my foster mum – and it's bad enough having to behave myself for those two without having to worry about a third!'

So it's all good. Well, apart from the time, shortly after Tyler joined the family, when we fostered a certain little girl. But that's another story, of course, to be told in another book …

Don't worry though. I won't keep you in suspense for long. ☺

CASEY WATSON

---

*One woman determined to
make a difference.*

*Read Casey's poignant
memoirs and be inspired.*

Five-year-old Justin was desperate and helpless

Six years after being taken into care, Justin has had 20 failed placements. Casey and her family are his last hope.

THE BOY NO ONE LOVED

A damaged girl haunted by her past

Sophia pushes Casey to the limits, threatening the safety of the whole family. Can Casey make a difference in time?

CRYING FOR HELP

SUNDAY TIMES BESTSELLING AUTHOR

CASEY WATSON

Little Prisoners

A tragic story of siblings trapped in a world of abuse and suffering

Abused siblings who do not know what it means to be loved

With new-found security and trust, Casey helps Ashton and Olivia to rebuild their lives.

LITTLE PRISONERS

SUNDAY TIMES BESTSELLING AUTHOR

CASEY WATSON

Too Hurt to Stay

The true story of a troubled boy's desperate search for a loving home

Branded 'vicious and evil', eight-year-old Spencer asks to be taken into care

Casey and her family are disgusted: kids aren't born evil. Despite the challenges Spencer brings, they are determined to help him find a loving home.

TOO HURT TO STAY

A young girl secretly caring for her mother

Abigail has been dealing with pressures no child should face. Casey has the difficult challenge of helping her to learn to let go.

A heartrending story of a child secretly caring for her severely disabled mother

Mummy's Little Helper

CASEY WATSON

SUNDAY TIMES BESTSELLING AUTHOR

MUMMY'S LITTLE HELPER

SUNDAY TIMES BESTSELLING AUTHOR

CASEY WATSON

Breaking the Silence

Two little boys, lost and unloved. One woman determined to make a difference

Two boys with an unlikely bond

With Georgie and Jenson, Casey is facing her toughest test yet.

BREAKING THE SILENCE

CASEY WATSON

A Last Kiss For Mummy

A teenage
mum, a
tiny infant,
a terrible
choice

A teenage mother and baby
in need of a loving home

At fourteen, Emma is just a child herself –
and one who's never been properly mothered.

A LAST KISS FOR MUMMY

CASEY WATSON

SUNDAY TIMES BESTSELLING AUTHOR

The Girl Without a Voice

The true story
of a terrified child
whose silence
spoke volumes

Book 1
of Casey's
teaching
memoirs

What is the secret behind Imogen's silence?

Discover the shocking and devastating past of a child
with severe behavioural problems.

THE GIRL WITHOUT A VOICE

FEEL HEART.
FEEL HOPE.
READ CASEY.